WILDERNESS
SHELTERS

AND HOW TO BUILD THEM

WILDERNESS
SHELTERS
AND HOW TO BUILD THEM

*A Fully Illustrated Guide to Log Cabins,
Shelters, and Wilderness Housekeeping*

BRADFORD ANGIER

ILLUSTRATED BY ELVENA ANGIER

LYONS
PRESS

Essex, Connecticut

An imprint of Globe Pequot, the trade division of
The Rowman & Littlefield Publishing Group, Inc.
4501 Forbes Blvd., Ste. 200
Lanham, MD 20706
www.rowman.com

Distributed by NATIONAL BOOK NETWORK

Copyright © 2001 by The Rowman & Littlefield Publishing Group, Inc.
Copyright © 1952 by Bradford Angier
Originally published in 1952 by Sheridan House as *How to Build Your Home in the Woods*

New Lyons Press paperback edition 2023

British Library Cataloguing in Publication Information available

Library of Congress Cataloging-in-Publication Data available

ISBN 978-1-4930-7716-8 (paperback)

♾™ The paper used in this publication meets the minimum requirements of American National Standard for Information Sciences—Permanence of Paper for Printed Library Materials, ANSI/NISO Z39.48-1992.

To our companions of many a campfire,
Charlie *and* Beth Brent.

CONTENTS

WILDERNESS
SHELTERS
AND HOW TO BUILD THEM

CHAPTER ONE

LOG CABINS, UNLIMITED

Anyone can build a log cabin. No special skill, such as axmanship, is needed. Logs can easily be squared into position by saw alone.

Log construction has been called costly. Yet one of the cabins described in these pages was built by one man in three days for less than two dollars. Windows can be installed with lumberjack finesse for the price of the glass alone. Trappers have a number of ways of making stoves at no expense other than that of pipe.

The wool-shirted pioneers who hewed log houses out of the North American wilderness were, for a large part, inexperienced men, working in a maximum of haste with a minimum of tools. If there had been anything complex about log work, they would have turned to some other type of building.

Log cabins, Unlimited, are still at the disposal of poor and rich, weak and strong, inept and skilled alike.

The folly of "spending the best part of one's life earning money in order to enjoy a questionable liberty during the least valuable part of it," was ridiculed by Henry David Thoreau who elected to make his home in the woods over a century ago.

If one hears the insistent call of the frontier, why shall he not answer it as fully as he may while eyes are still keen and stride lusty?

Scientists remind us that nature intended that human beings should spend most of their hours beneath open skies. With appetites sharpened by robust living, they should eat plain foods. They should live at self-regulated paces, unoppressed by the artificial hurry and tension of man-made civilization.

Yet, as Thoreau pointed out, the mass of men lead lives of quiet desperation. They make themselves sick that they may lay up something against a sick day. Their incessant anxiety is a well-nigh incurable form of disease.

"All summer I've heard pilgrims enthusing, 'Oh, heaven!' " one of a group of woodsmen grunted when I was heading outside one fall by ship from Skagway, Alaska. "But every time I see their cities again, all I can think is, 'Oh, hell.' "

The Pursuit of Happiness

The happiest man I know dwells in a log cabin on the sunny north bank of the Peace River, over 100 miles from where the last railway steel ends and three miles from his nearest neighbor.

Years ago, as a cabinet maker's apprentice in an English city, Dudley Shaw used to trudge several miles after work on many evenings for a few free minutes of fishing. He came to his decision one dusk. When unspoiled spaces beckoned, why should he waste the vigorous years of his life merely snatching at fragmentary pleasure?

At present in his spruce castle in the Canadian Rockies, what is he but a king? He runs a short trap line in winter to give him the odd $200 he needs to live, royally, for another year. He is past 70, but there is a youthfulness in his walk and a zest in his smile that are lacking in many a city man of 30.

Whereas, the latter often only exists, my friend lives—breathing clean air, beholden to none, doing what he wants most to do and giving it his best.

My Log Cabin

For several delightful years, I have been his "nearest neighbor."

My log cabin stands near the edge of a cliff where swooping swallows build grey colonies of gourd-like nests. A mountain brook sparkles by my front door before hurling itself in a diamond torrent to the wilderness river below.

Jade slopes, fragrant with spruce, cup the land in sheltered solitude. Down river are the smokes of the closest settlement where, six miles along a pleasant trail, a handful of log cabins cluster lazily around a Hudson's Bay Company trading post.

I can eat my oatmeal—on mornings when the breeze is sweet with silver willow—watching black cow moose at the river's edge with their tiny tan calves. Many a winter's dinner is interrupted by the sight of yellow coyotes and great dark Siberian wolves following the river's icy trail.

Freedoms

A coal oil lamp is the only "electricity" in this particular cabin, a pair of pails the water system. There were other simplicities, too. Well, maybe some folks would call them inconveniences. They're also freedoms from responsibility. If you don't have running water, there's no worry about frozen, bursting pipes. If your coal heater runs on your own wood, strikes and other fuel difficulties are something to plague the other fellow.

Reading is an important part of log cabin living. Publications are never allowed to become old, for here one has time to do the things he wants. Local bushmen are far more soundly in touch with world problems than the average subway or bus chaser. Interpretations of international trends are painstakingly restudied . . . a year or two after the prophecies have, or have not, come to pass! Some highly paid commentators don't rate pennies along the Peace River.

Sustenance

Besides joining in the butchering of some seers' reputations, we run our own meat shops. The forest furnishes moose tenderloins, bear kidneys, and venison chops. The mountains proffer sheep and goat roasts. There are lynx steaks and plump young beavers, too. Even wolf isn't half bad.

Fish are free for the fun of catching. Arctic grayling and flysocking rainbow trout rise eagerly to Black Gnats. There are muskies and wall-eyes, too. A lazy man doesn't even have to bother with such piscatory pleasures. Unattended night lines brought their quota of Dolly Vardens and vitamin-rich ling . . . the freshwater cod that ichthyologists call "living fossils."

Spring arrives with a rush. Honking geese, ducks, and glistening white swans cloud blue skies. One can stand in an aspen grove on a warm spring morning and actually hear leaves busting open like popcorn. Vegetables grow to record proportions during sunny days so long that one can read outdoors at midnight. Nearly everyone has his own garden.

Wild fruits and vegetables are abundant. One stuffs himself joyously in a vain effort to keep abreast of the supply. Amaranth proves tastier than the choicest market greens. Willow shoots impart a celery-like flavor to soups. Fireweed stalks are the backwoods asparagus.

One can brew tea from spruce needles, from spicy yarrow flowers, and from the bark of birch roots. Dried dandelion roots, ground and roasted, made a creditable coffee. Most visiting sportsmen try shredding the inner bark of the flowering dogwood for cigarettes. This is the so-called "kinnikinnik" of local trappers, smoked in these mountains for centuries.

Vacations

Not all may heed the summons of the open places. But many who believe themselves chained to civilized tasks are held only by inertia, environment, and lack of self-confidence.

Suppose one truly has but weekends or a fortnight yearly when he may do what he really wants?

The best vacation a city man can have, said Horace Kephart the great woodsman and writer, is to go where he can build his own shelter, secure and cook his own food, do his own chores, and thereby, in some measure, discover anew those lost arts of wildcraft that were our heritage through centuries past but which not one modern man in a hundred knows anything at all about.

Preparations

Erect your own shelter! Something about building a wilderness home takes you close to the beginning of things. An atavism it is; a throw-back, dulled by years of apartment living, but none the less vital for all that. The instinctive hut-building ardor of any small boy is the proof.

Even if you do not plan to start building right away, you will be missing one of the sweetest pleasures of all if you don't begin preparations now. You'll be passing up the pulse-quickening, fancy-luring joy of making plans, of purposely thumbing books and maps, and of drawing queer designs with stubby pencils on pads carried for the time when inspiration comes.

Start Now

There is still room in the world for those who prefer the "unimproved works of God" to man-made cities. If you would join the procession back to the land, may I add one personal remark. My only regret has been that I put it off so long.

"Yesterday is ashes, tomorrow wood," the Indians say, "Only today does the fire burn brightly."

CHAPTER TWO

WHERE TO BUILD

"My dwelling was small, and I could hardly entertain an echo in it," Thoreau said when he took to the New England woods more than a century ago. "But it seemed larger for being a single apartment and remote from neighbors."

Where

Remoteness must be a major consideration, negative or positive, in the selection of a cabin location.

The week-ender needs a retreat within easy reach of his weekday home. Of prime importance to most, for that matter, is a site that can be readily reached in all weather by automobile.

Everyone desires essentials such as water, fuel, and sustenance to be quickly available. Then there are such matters as scenery, recreational opportunities, safety, climate, sunlight, cost, and resale value to take into personal account.

Modern Daniel Boones and Davy Crocketts, many of whom would have stayed cramped in cities if not jolted from their ruts by war, judge ideal accessibility from the opposite viewpoint. They want to laugh in farther places . . . where wild foods are free for the gathering, meat for the stalking, fuel for the cutting, and habitation for the joy of building.

Aquatics

"It is well to have some water in your neighborhood," Thoreau thought. "It is earth's eye, looking into which the beholder measures the depth of his own nature."

Rivers and lakes are roads for that unrivaled pack horse and pleasure craft, the canoe. Even the tiniest brook may be dammed to form a bathing pool. The air currents, conditioned by water, are reservoirs of coolness in summer, dispersers of pests during fly seasons. Streams in winter become ice-paved highways. Water's contribution to beauty and serenity is inestimable; its liquid chatter a constant companion. To be avoided, of course, are such shortcomings as a site that may be ringed by swamps in spring, flooded during wet seasons, or stranded far from receding banks during dry months. Unless one particularly admires the high wooden sidewalks of the pioneer town and wishes to construct similar routes, the ground should drain freely.

Visualization

It may be easier to visualize the future home if its proposed outline is marked by stakes and string. One may then examine the location from all angles, externally and internally, and ask innumerable questions about sunlight, shade, wind, drainage, view, and every other consideration that comes to mind. If the answers are not satisfactory, it will be an easy matter at this stage to move the stakes and test other possibilities until the best site is found.

Selection

How does one select a wilderness niche? A search of the countryside within convenient driving distance of one's home may turn the trick. Scanning maps and talking to acquaintances "who've been there" may be a help, too. Voluminous information may be obtained by writing to the tourist bureaus that are located in state and provincial capitals.

You may state your problem to the Department of the Interior in Washington, D. C., and to the Government Travel Bureau in Ottawa, Ontario. Letters to leading outdoor magazines bring frank, surprisingly painstaking suggestions. The tourist representatives of most railroads are also well supplied with details.

Adjectives will be necessarily discounted. Conclusions will be drawn from temperature charts, forestry reports, contour maps, rainfall tables, graphs of frost-free periods, botanical lists, wildlife surveys, and other concrete factors.

Legalities

Anyone buying land wants to be sure that he obtains clear title and, unless the area is on a public road, a right of way to it. It is good insurance to have professional assistance in this matter.

The common procedure, after a verbal agreement has been reached, is for its terms to be put on paper and signed by both seller and buyer. The vendor promises to deliver a certain piece of property on a definite day. The purchaser, who generally makes a small payment at once as evidence of good faith, agrees to accept delivery at that time and to pay as agreed.

The waiting period between the moment of the agreement and the actual sale allows both parties time in which to get any necessary affairs in order. The purchaser owes it to himself to examine the title and to verify the boundaries even to the extent of having them surveyed if necessary.

The reason for searching the title is to make sure that it is owned undisputedly by the seller and that, unless otherwise specified, it is free of encumbrances. Among these may be building restrictions, such as zoning laws, and easements which are privileges given some outside party, as for instance a right of way accorded a power company or municipality.

A local lawyer will usually investigate the title for a small fee, and it is generally advisable to secure such aid. Assistance may also be secured in some cases from county and state registry offices, from a local bank, particularly if a mortgage is being sought there, and occasionally from one's own real estate agent.

The deed to secure if possible is the warranty type, in which the seller and his heirs make themselves liable to defend the title to date of sale from any claims or litigation. A quit claim deed, the other variety, is self explanatory. The seller merely passes over to the buyer any and all rights he may have in the property. It is often a wise precaution to insure the title with a title guaranty insurance company.

If a bank loan is arranged for the property, the bank will make sure of all necessary details for its own protection. The bank in this instance generally acts for a set fee as escrow holder. It holds the purchase money, in other words, until all terms of the written agreement between buyer and seller are fulfilled to its satisfaction, relieving the purchaser of burdensome technical details.

Once the deed has been transferred to the new owner, the latter should affix Documentary Tax Stamps and for his own protection should record the transaction in the local registry office.

Public Lands

Log cabin sites innumerable are provided in the national parks of the United States and Canada for lease fees running upward from $8 yearly in the Dominion and generally ranging from $15 to $25 per annum in Uncle Sam's domains.

More than 13,000 private homes already nestle in national forests, stretching from Alaska to Puerto Rico, administered by the U. S. Forest Service. The fact that this is scarcely a handful is better appreciated when one realizes these public woodlands cover more than 176 million acres—over an acre apiece for every man, woman, and child in the country.

Canada's some 18 million acres of national park land, sheltering less than a thousand private dwellings, afford a wide choice of sites for the modern frontiersman who would erect his wilderness home where the "good old days" that sportsmen dream about still exist.

U. S. Park Sites

Since a private home is an exclusive use of national forest land, the United States Department of Agriculture holds that it must not be allowed to conflict with public usages. There are thousands of square miles to chose from, however. The foresters' natural object is to locate the dwellings in attractive, suitable, and conveniently reached country with good forest cover.

"Summer homes do not require a large area," the Forest Service notes, "and places can be found which are very satisfactory for summer homes and yet do not interfere with public use. Such areas are surveyed into lots or units of one-half to one acre in size."

The only regulations governing the building and use of private homes are those held to be necessary to guard the administive principle—the greatest good to the greatest number for the greatest length of time.

Special restrictions vary with local conditions. The main rules are the following: Architectural and constructional standards must be met. The locations of buildings, all of which must harmonize with the forest environment, have to be approved by the forest officer in charge. Sanitation facilities need to conform with State and National Forest requirements.

Private homes may not be used commercially except by special permission. Subleasing, which will not be formally approved as a general practice, should have the forest supervisor's confirmation. Transfer of ownership may not be negotiated except by government permit. Premises must be well maintained. All game and fire laws must, of course, be observed.

Specific details about available home sites may be secured from the supervisor of the particular forest in which the individual is interested and from the United States Forest Service, Department of Agriculture, Washington, D. C.

Canada's National Parks

The National Parks Bureau, Department of Mines and Resources, Ottawa, Ontario, performs a similar function in Canada. Canada's eleven million inhabitants are largely bulked near the U. S. border, leaving, virtually untrod, hundreds of thousands of square miles, the final reservoir of many a record big-game trophy.

Town sites have been laid out in appropriate spots throughout the Dominion's fertile maze of national forests that extend from the salty Atlantic Coast of Nova Scotia to the Selkirk Mountains of British Columbia. Lots vary in size, fifty feet frontage by twice that depth being the usual minimum. Necessary regulations, similar to those across the border, are in effect. Building materials and plans must be approved by the National Parks Bureau.

Alaska's Free Land

Alaska is so new and big—nearly as large as the United States, east of the Mississippi—that nobody's spoiled it yet. There isn't even an income tax! Alaskan land is free to anyone who's an American citizen or has declared his intention to become one. If the head of a family, that individual does not even have to be 21 years old.

No one need worry about the best sites having already been picked. Alaska's 75,000 regular inhabitants, half of whom are natives, wouldn't fill the Rose Bowl at Pasadena, Calif. There are roughly 225,000,000 Alaskan acres subject to disposal under public land laws. That's nearly two-thirds of a vast and vacant empire which is twice as large as Texas.

Alaskan Climate

Climate needn't keep anyone back, either. Southeastern Alaska, for example, is virtually as mild as Virginia. The regions along the polar sea are the only ones where Arctic conditions prevail.

Arctic conditions? The U. S. Weather Bureau bears out the fact that it actually gets 10° colder in popular Yellowstone National Park than at Barrow, on Alaska's northernmost tip. Everlasting winter? A 100° in the shade has been recorded at Fort Yukon, north of the Arctic Circle.

Blizzards are actually unknown in many sections. More snow falls in Chicago during an average winter than in numerous northern localities. Chinooks—hot, dry west winds—periodically evaporate drifts in part, of the continental corner, zooming temperatures in my experience more than 70° in a single hour.

Even in the frosty interior of Alaska, thermometers drop little, if any, lower than in Montana and Wyoming. Elsewhere, they're often surprisingly higher. The average January temperature of such an American city as Minneapolis is 13°. Compare that to such January averages in Alaska as 22° in Seward, 27° in Juneau, 29° in Wrangell, and 32° in Ketchikan and Sitka.

If servicemen have been heard bewailing "a rocky, treeless country with the worst climate in the world," they were talking about the Aleutians. Even these raw, foggy islands may be oases for sheep men and fur raisers. An island less than 30 square miles an area may be leased by a prospective fur farmer for $50 a year.

"A body jest nat'rally can't explain Alaska's climate in a couple of words," says sourdough prospector Jack Adams who came North in gold-rush days. "Why, if Alaska was laid atop the States, it'd stretch from Canada to Mexico, and from South Carolina to Californy."

Alaskan Homesteads

There's still enough free land in Alaska to make 290 states the size of Rhode Island. The most popular method of obtaining a share is by homesteading.

"There are two ways of initiating a claim under homestead laws," advises the General Land Office in Washington, D. C. "One is by making a settlement; that is, actually going upon the land with the intention of using it for a home. The other is by filing an application for a homestead entry at the appropriate district land office."

District Land Offices in Alaska are at Fairbanks, Anchorage, and Nome. Information about free land may be obtained from them and from the General Land Office in Washington, D. C. Land is available in the national forests, too. The U. S. Forest Service at Juneau, Alaska, will supply information about this.

A homesteader may secure title to as much as 160 acres by living on the land not less than seven months annually for three years, building a home thereon, and putting at least one-eighth of the area under cultivation.

One may file on newly opened land 90 days ahead of the general public if honorably discharged after 90 days or more of military service.

"Such qualified ex-servicemen are also eligible to have a period equal to their term of service, up to two years, deducted from the three years' residence required under homestead laws," says the General Land Office. "This means that for those entitled to the maximum credit, the actual residence need only be seven months. Only one-16th of the land will then have to be put under cultivation."

A lot of folks won't want to homestead, of course. There are other ways of gaining title or use of Alaska's public land. Free five-acre homesites will interest many.

Money up North

How about earning a living? Opportunities litter the Alaskan landscape. If ever a time was tailor-made in Alaska for Americans eager to strike out on their own, it's now. As the case always has been on any frontier, most of these Alaskan opportunities are for hustlers with pioneer hardihood and hearts for adventure.

All right, so you can take nature in the raw. You can thrive on isolation, log cabin towns, and unpaved streets lighted only by the Aurora Borealis. What are your chances?

If you'd like to have a job waiting, perhaps you can land what you want by mail. Queries about private Alaskan positions may be addressed to the U. S. Employment Service at Seattle, Washington. The Alaska Railroad, also with offices in Seattle, is on the lookout for railroad workers. The 11th Civil Service District in Seattle should be contacted regarding civil service openings.

For information about aviation, write the Civil Aeronautics Administration in Washington, D. C. War Department projects are under the supervision of the Overseas Branch, Office of the Secretary of War, Washington, D. C. The Alaska Road Commission at Juneau, Alaska, hires construction and maintenance men.

Have you enough capital to go in business for yourself? Alaska may well be the Promised Land for the right sort of individual with $1000, $5000, or $15,000, asserts Ernest Gruening, the Territorial Governor, who points out that such a man, by mixing his money with brains, can make his pile much faster than in a more developed country.

The sensational progress made in Alaskan transportation is an example of what can happen. The Territory's population remained stagnant for 30 years because virtually the only travel to and from the outside world was by slow, expensive sea passage. Alaska is now linked overland with the outside by the Alaska Highway. It has suddenly been recognized as the most central place in the world of aircraft.

From Seattle to Calcutta, over Alaska, it's 4,775 miles shorter than the old ocean route. It is no wonder experts are repeating the late General William Mitchell's words: "Whoever holds Alaska will hold the world."

Fairbanks is the hub of an aerial wheel that rings the industrial centers of the globe. It's 3,300 miles from this northern terminus of the Alaska Highway to New York, 3,500 to Tokio, 4,100 to Moscow, and 4,200 to London.

Room for Pioneers

Life in Alaska is simple and satisfying if one has the frontier spirit. A log home may be had for the building. Firewood in most sections is free for the cutting. There are mountain goat, sheep, deer, caribou, and the largest moose and bear in the world. Millions of succulent game birds, some migrating from Asia and Europe, wing the skies. A resident hunting license costs $2.

Wild potatoes and onions are free for the digging, wild rice for the harvesting, great juicy fruits for the plucking, birch sugar for the distilling, wild tea and coffee for the drying, and atamaoya and other native tobaccos for the fun of finding.

How about youngsters? Modern schools, as well as churches and hospitals, are in all the larger towns. Rural schools are widely distributed. Free college tuition is afforded residents by the highly rated University of Alaska which offers regular four-year courses in everything from pre-medicine and business administration to arts and letters.

The world still has room for pioneers.

Formula

"At a certain season of our life we are accustomed to consider every spot as the possible site of a house," Thoreau noted. He recommended Cato's yardstick. "The oftener you go there the more it will please you, if it is good!"

CHAPTER THREE

TIMBER-R-R-R!

Too many today take an occasional wistful look at log cabins and sadly vow that ax work is not for them. The happy fact is that *no ax is required* for the construction of a wilderness home.

Logs can be notched into position by saw and hammer, or a chisel and mallet will do the job. It is true, however, that

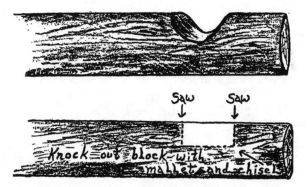

No ax is needed for log cabin building. Saw and chisel may be used instead.

ax-made joints are far less difficult than they appear. A major reason why many an individual distrusts his axmanship is because the woodpile weapon to which he's accustomed is duller than a butterknife.

Anyone who is able to swing a hammer and ply a saw can

build a good log cabin. The job is not painstaking. There are not even any set and fixed rules. Constructing a warm, sturdy, and presentable log cabin is far less complicated than putting up a satisfactory frame dwelling.

The Start

Frame houses may start with foundations. In the case of log cabins, however, it's best to fell the sticks at the first. The logs can then be drying while one goes ahead with other basic work.

The seasoned building wood, like the pre-shrunk fabric, is insurance against later toil and trouble. This does not mean that undried sticks are not used every day. Problems presented by subsequent shrinkage are greater, that is all. More extended and extensive chinking is required, for one thing.

Logs, like human beings, become progressively leaner while dehydrating. Their lengths remain the same.

Seasoning

To dry properly logs should be piled, preferably, at least one foot off the ground on skids. Skids are merely two logs laid at right angles to the pile.

The logs should be separated throughout so that all parts will be ventilated. Shade is preferable to sunshine for the first month or two, unless haste is necessary. This may be assured, if no better means are available, by covering the pile lightly with evergreen boughs. It is advisable to turn the logs every month or so. A quarter-turn each time will give results superior to those achieved by half-turns.

Logs so handled will, if felled shortly after the first hard frost, be suitable for ordinary building purposes the next spring. A full year's seasoning is better.

Seasoning On The Stump

Bushmen often cannot be bothered by waiting for logs to dry and use sticks as they fell them. They generally hunt out sound, standing dead wood for key logs in such instances. Such wood has seasoned on the stump.

Many such logs are provided by fire-killed trees. These can too often be found in unfortunate quantities that, peeled and then scrubbed with sand if necessary, present hard white surfaces.

Cutting

Building logs may be cut and used at any time, but there are certain practices that are advantageous to follow. Winter felling is preferable. Most sticks season better when brought down in cold weather and peeled in the spring. Danger of insect injury is also less then. Snow, too, acts as a protective cushion for the crashing timber.

Even the greenest cheechako or newcomer can safely drop large trees in the general direction he chooses if he will observe the few simple principles that are explained in the next chapter.

An established price in some of the remoter backwoods localities for felling, peeling, and delivering sticks of specified dimensions has long been a dollar or two a log. Where trees grow straight, enough for a cabin can easily be dropped in a day.

Fifty or one hundred dollars thus spent on sticks, averaging from eight to ten inches in diameter, will place on skids, ready for use, the logs necessary for the ordinary cabin. Such costs, unfortunately, rise sharply the nearer one is to what is most politely called civilization.

Help

A sagacious old timer may often be hired for several dollars a day, if one will let word spread. He will punctuate expert ax strokes with apt suggestions and acceptable recommendations.

Before rolling in to his blankets beside the campfire, likely as not he'll charm his listeners with tales . . . such as how John Hornby trapped the Barren Lands one winter from living quarters in an abandoned wolf den; and how Twelve-Foot Davis, late at a gold stampede, found an error in location measurements and staked himself a 144-inch strip in the center of the workings from which he took a fortune in yellow metal.

Cabin Logs

The usual log cabin seldom takes more than fifty or sixty logs. The pick of available timber should certainly be used, therefore.

Care exerted in its selection will be very much worth the trouble.

Logs from six to twelve inches in average diameter are a good general size. If a stick is eight inches through at one end and ten inches thick at the other, its average diameter is the total of both measurements divided by two—that is, nine inches.

The larger sticks are eminently satisfactory, particularly for the more pretentious structure, but their weights make them harder to handle. The same consideration applies to lengths which, particularly when they are being managed by novices, may well be limited to about twenty-five feet.

Taper

The slighter the taper, the easier the work! The sticks will be alternated, butts for tops throughout, to compensate for tapering.

Walls may be kept reasonably level, that is, by laying one tier of logs clockwise butt to top, butt to top, butt to top, and butt to top. The next tier of the rectangle, also viewed clockwise, will run top to butt, top to butt, top to butt, and top to butt.

Uniformity

If a nearly uniform set of wall logs can be assembled, the task of keeping the rising sides approximately level and plumb will be considerably lessened.

Uniformity is fortunately not necessary for it is not always possible. When diameters vary markedly, some builders capitalize on the discrepancy by putting up particularly graceful walls that are stoutest at the base and which diminish gradually as they ascend.

Poles

The fact that only small poles may be available can serve to make cabin construction even easier. The frame is put up first in such instances. The poles, sawed to a common length, are nailed between flattened sills and plates as shown in the accompanying illustration.

This palisade style is actually so effective that full-sized logs are often utilized in the same manner. Some particularly appealing wilderness homes combine both motifs. Sticks are set horizon-

Side of pole house, showing how to frame windows, doors, and corners.

tally throughout, for example, except for vertical panels above windows and doors and at gables.

Species

One should pick the soundest, straightest growth at hand. This varies in different sections. Evergreens on the whole provide the most popular building logs throughout the United States and Canada. Cedar, balsam, tamarack, fir, pine, hemlock, redwood, and spruce are all good.

Some other woods, such as oak and chestnut have to be seasoned, then hewn into shape if the cabin is not to resemble latticework.

Quickly deteriorating species—as for example cottonwood, buckeye, basswood, willow, and aspen—are not practical. If they must be employed, high and well ventilated foundations are mandatory to protect them from dampness.

Cedar is particularly advantageous for pillars, furniture, and for general decorative purposes. It also makes ground-embedded posts difficult to excel. Osage orange has similar vigorous durability. So does locust, cypress, redwood, and chestnut.

Iron oak resists ground decay and is a prime foundation and post wood. So is juniper. Birch, although too prone to rot to be used as cabin logs, is widely prized for furniture because of its adaptability and beauty.

Transporting

Logs not felled at the building site are most satisfactorily and inexpensively transported by waterways. If they are hauled by team, snow will ease the task and protect the sticks.

Log boats are superior to chains for drags of any distance. Sticks that are to be used unpeeled should not be subjected to the abrading effect of drag chains.

Peeling

Peeled logs last longer, deter everlastingly tunneling insects, and assure a brighter and cleaner cabin. Bark peels readily from most trees when the sap becomes fluid in the spring. The procedure is first to hew or shave a thin strip from the log along its en-

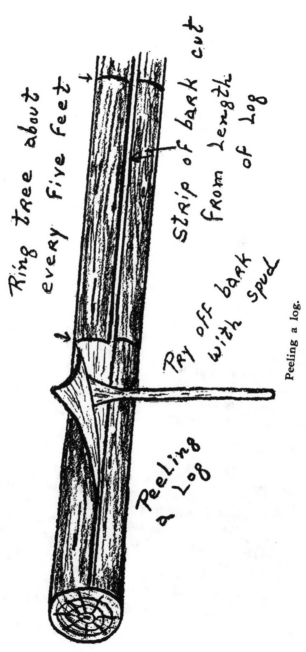

Ring tree about every five feet

Strip of bark cut from length of log

Pry off bark with spud

Peeling a Log

Peeling a log.

31

tire length. The bark is then pried off in great rolls by inserting a spud between bark and trunk.

The spud is a bushman's chisel that may be whittled from a piece of hardwood in a few minutes. It has no set dimensions, inasmuch as individual preferences vary. A convenient size for barking is a slim wedge-shaped head, about three inches wide, at the end of a two-foot handle.

Trees peeled when the sap is dormant must be drawshaved or otherwise laboriously stripped. Such timber as the soft pine has to be so treated at all times. A few trees, like the cedar, are functional with the bark left on.

Bark

Many backwoodsmen save the bark thus obtained for such building purposes as shingling roofs and sheathing gables. The bark is first flattened under pressure. One hinterland trick is to season it in sand for several months.

It was written of Massachusetts Indians back in 1674, a little more than a half century after the Pilgrims had landed there: "The best of their houses are covered very neatly, tight and warm, with the barks of trees, slipped from their bodies at those seasons when the sap is up, and made into great flakes, with pressure of weighty timber, when they are green. . . . Some I have seen, sixty or a hundred feet long and thirty feet broad."

Unpeeled

Logs that are to be used unpeeled are best felled when the sap is inactive. Dropping them as soon as practicable after the first heavy frost will allow a maximum of time for seasoning.

It is a sound practice to protect unpeeled logs against insect damage by felling the timber in cold weather and then brushing hot creosote immediately over all cuts. This treatment with the coal tar product, about which more appears elsewhere, should be repeated shortly before the sticks are used.

The bark will adhere more tightly if a strip is removed from the top and bottom of each stick along its entire length. The longitudinal scores may later be hidden between the walls.

Tacking on the bark with large-headed nails of inconspicuous color will do much to prevent a future bedraggled appearance. One fastener for every square foot of surface is usually enough. In other words, using unpeeled logs in the wilderness home is usually a whole lot more trouble than the results justify. A common sequel is awkward peeling and refinishing when the sticks are in place.

Checking

If one objects to the cracks that open in logs as they dry, this checking may be lessened slightly and localized largely.

Logs felled in the fall and placed unpeeled on skids may have narrow strips of bark cut from the full length of their two opposite sides. This scoring will increase the adhesion of the remaining bark which, when one is particular, is sometimes temporarily tacked at about every square foot to the trunk.

Checking, which is practically bound to appear somewhere, will then generally occur along the exposed and therefore dryer surfaces. The peeling may be completed in the spring and the creviced sides later largely hidden by the cabin chinking. Care should be taken to keep the newly felled logs out of direct sunlight for at least two months, as too rapid drying is a cause of excessive checking.

Further checking can be discouraged by brushing the peeled but unshaven log with boiled linseed oil. When this dries, (a process that can be speeded by first diluting the oil with one-fourth its volumn of turpentine,) a coat of the clear oil may be applied.

Third and fourth coats are sometimes given to further the effectiveness of this treatment which not only discourages checking, but adds to the longevity of the sticks by holding on the cambium. The cambium is the connective soft tissue between the bark and heartwood, prone to dry and disintegrate with age.

Most bushmen, frankly, don't bother one way or another about checking except occasionally to fill a particularly wide fissure with clay plaster or other chinking. The most harmonious material ordinarily used for this purpose is sawdust mixed with melted sheet glue.

Preservatives

Beetles, borers, and their brethren cause damage and annoyance in some localities, particularly if the log or slab is left unpeeled. A few local inquiries will let one know what to expect.

A good rule in such vicinities is to fell the trees after the first heavy frost and to lay them at once in well ventilated position on skids, turning each stick periodically.

Such durable species as cedar, juniper, cypress, and redwood are usually immune even though summer-felled, if the tops are detached and the logs laid separately and turned at least three times at weekly intervals. It is well to use such naturally resistant woods whenever practicable in infected areas.

Creosote

Unpeeled wood may be protected to some extent, when necessary, by brushing at least the bare parts and, preferably, the entire surface with a solution of one part of creosote and three parts of kerosene by volume, then allowing it to dry in the sun.

The brush employed should either be one manufactured especially for work with creosote or a regular paint applicator whose bristles have been reinforced by being wound with wire. Too, a discarded small broom with soft bristles is frequently retrieved for the task. First grade, liquid oil, coal tar creosote should be used if one does not wish to stain the wood too darkly.

Peeled logs may be similarly handled advantageously if the vicinity where one is building calls for such precautions.

Troughs are sometimes constructed of galvanized iron, or made by cutting and welding a series of 55-gallon drums, and all wood immersed in the solution of creosote and kerosene before being dried and used for building.

Pyridine

Crude pyridine, which can also be diluted by three parts of kerosene, may be substituted for creosote. It may also be applied either by brush or by dip. Pyridine has the advantage of being colorless.

Penta

Pentachlorophenol will guard logs and lumber against termites, powder-post beetles, and similar pests. Proper application will also protect wood from the fungi which thrive on warmth, air, moisture, and food—the latter being, unfortunately, the wood itself—the process known as rotting.

One part of "penta" crystals by weight is dissolved in nineteen parts of petroleum oil. The heavier fuel and lubricating oils are recommended for damp locations and for wood which will be in contact with the ground. Used crankcase oil may be employed to keep down expenses if appearance is not a factor. "Penta," ineffective on green materials, is readily absorbed by such seasoned woods as pine. It may be applied by any of the usual brushing, spraying, swabbing, soaking, and dipping methods.

Bush Methods

A quick and inexpensive bush method, particularly applicable to such green logs as poplar, is to burn quickly flaring birch bark or dry evergreen boughs beneath them, forcing them to produce their own creosote. If one wants clean bright logs, however, this backwoods kink has its obvious drawbacks.

Drastic Measures

Wood already attacked by beetles and borers can be treated with a solution of nine parts of turpentine and one of kerosene.

More drastically, it can be thoroughly sprayed or brushed by crude orthodichlorobenzene which has been diluted by eight parts of kerosene. This colorless liquid is slightly poisonous and should be applied outdoors or in a well ventilated building. Incidentally, it will kill vegetation on contact.

Care should be taken to keep it, pyridine, and creosote off the skin and out of eyes. Goggles and rubber gloves are recommended for any overhead work.

Paradichlorobenzene may be used similarly. It is sold in white crystals which for this work should be dissolved in three parts of kerosene by weight.

Finalities

Building will progress more happily if all logs are segregated before any are used. The straightest, soundest, and sturdiest one will be reserved for the ridgepole. Piled to one side with it will be such carefully selected key sticks as the sills, joists, and purlins.

A number of extra logs should be at hand. Then if a mistake is made, the cabin owner can reach composedly for an alternate and relegate the original nonchalantly to the woodpile.

"Shall we," asked Thoreau, "forever resign the pleasure of construction to the carpenter?"

CHAPTER FOUR

DON'T BE AN EXPERT

"Near the end of March 1845, I cut down some tall pines by Walden Pond and hewed timbers, studs and rafters with my axe," wrote Henry David Thoreau. "By the middle of April, for I made no haste in my work but rather the most of it, my house was ready for raising.

"I dug my cellar in the side of a hill where a woodchuck had formerly dug his burrow, down through sumach and blackberry roots. In May, with the help of acquaintances—rather to improve so good an occasion for neighborliness than from any necessity —I set up the frame of my house and as soon as it was boarded and roofed, I began to occupy it."

Thoreau's home in the woods cost him $28.12.

"I intend to build me a home that will surpass any on the main street in grandeur and luxury, as soon as it pleases me as much," he wrote, "and will cost me no more than my present one."

Felling

Even the greenest tenderfoot can fell his first trees in a given direction if he will follow the simple principles set forth here. Wind, incline, weight, and surrounding objects must of course be taken into consideration.

A small safety notch is first made to minimize any possibility of the butt's kicking back or the trunk's splitting. Below this on the opposite side, where the tree is to fall, a wide notch is cut. When this indentation is about three-fifths through, a few strokes at the first nick should send the tree crashing.

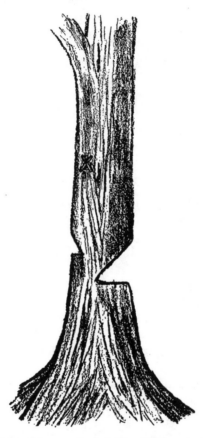

Safety-hinge principle for felling trees.

The two notches are so placed that they form a natural hinge. This hinge controls the direction of the fall and lessens the chance that the butt may thrust backward. However, one should have his eye on a safe place and should hurry there when the moment comes for the call of "Timber-r-r-r!"

Saw

The saw is used in a similar fashion; a brief cut, a deep slit opposite and below, and the subsequent deepening of the first incision. An ax or a wedge, perhaps one cut on the spot, may have to be driven into the lower gash to free the saw.

The right kind of saw resolves felling and cutting into a relative pastime. The long Swedish type blade is prefered by many. Its sharp thinness speeds through wood with a minimum of exertion. Its lightness makes it easy to manipulate horizontally. The limber steel itself can be coiled to the width of a saucer and tied with twine wound between its teeth for transporting. The two-part handle is also easily disjointed and carried. In an emergency, a stout green sapling can be bent into use as a frame.

The cranky side of a swede saw is its disposition to twist and bind. Many select the heavier, comparatively rigid crosscut saw for this reason. The crosscut is of particular value in cabin construction for making the straight cuts necessary for window and door openings. Besides being surer and steadier than the tempermental swede saw, it can be inserted in a wall in the space made by removing one log. The one-man crosscut, on which an additional handle can be slipped in an instant, will suffice.

Assistance

The actual felling and readying of the logs may be one task that the builder will want to have done for him. Several practical reasons may direct this decision, not the least of which may be the owner's inability to be conveniently on hand at the best times to drop, trim, transport, and peel the sticks. Costs for this work vary as suggested in the previous chapter but will generally be low, particularly if one will talk man-to-man to some conscientious old timer who's looking for a little extra work to occupy his hours.

The Ax

Paul Bunyan, the legendary lumberman, used to build up such a hunger wielding the familar woodpile weapon that it took a ton or two of dynamite to flip the massive flapjacks his appetite demanded.

Our ancestors who hewed two great countries out of the timbered vastness north of the Rio Grande understood ax work well.

The principles of the primitive art are known now but to a few. However, these fundamentals are as simple as ever.

The ax, rated by some experts as even more valuable than matches to the woodsman alone in the forest, is the tool most often slighted and abused by the cheechako. Yet the essentials of its use, being based on common sense, are easy to remember.

The builder of a wilderness home will probably want to make the ax his servant, although it should be emphasized again that anyone can build a log cabin without even touching an ax.

Name Your Weapon

Grizzled oldsters in frontier stores often peddle lumberjack's bludgeons innocently to one and all. The two-and-one-half or three pound head with about a twenty-eight inch handle is enough ax for most refugees from paved streets, although some may find they swing the thirty-six inch handle more naturally. A single cutting edge is sufficient.

The venerable broadax, a huge wide blade on a long bent handle, can flatten logs as smoothly as a plane when it is in the hands of those expert in using it. An adz is also a fine tool for this purpose, under similar circumstances.

Practically anyone can safely do satisfactory work, from hewing to notching, with a heavy broad hatchet. The short handle is easier for the novice to manipulate. Even experienced backwoods builders use such a hatchet, particularly in locations where it would be less convenient to swing a full sized ax.

The above very definitely does not refer to a belt ax, although a good one of these is useful to the camper if only to preserve his hunting or pocket knife blade. It simplifies butchering, occasionally eases fire making, and saves time in impromptu trail blazing. Its poor reputation stems from the fact that when it is used for heavy work, the belt ax is bouncy and jarring.

The handiest ax for packing, although not for general building, is the Hudson Bay type with narrow butt and regular-width face. An occasional painstaking craftsman employs it on cabins, but such an individual is generally an assiduous perfectionist who if he were working with milled stock would be a cabinetmaker rather than a carpenter. A one-and-one-half pound head with a twenty-four inch handle will fulfill ordinary camping requirements. A metal-riveted leather sheath should be added.

It is false economy to look for ax bargains. This is expressly true since well balanced, expertly tempered, and conscientiously forged brands may be purchased for a very few dollars.

Sharpness

A prime reason why many a man comes to distrust his axmanship is that the implement to which he is accustomed is about as sharp as an old hoe. A small carborundum or oilstone, supplemented with a flat file for use on nicks, holds the solution. Chisels, knives, and all keen-edged tools should be kept sharpened.

After one has labored over a blade several times, he will take care to avoid hard knots and other blunting substances.

Hot and Cold

Woodsmen may be seen on frosty mornings, warming axes in their hands. An ax left out during a frigid night may shiver to fragments at the first stoke. So may a chisel for that matter, while care must be taken not to bend a saw that has become brittle with frosts, as I learned one morning during a 100°-below-freezing hiatus in the sub-Arctic.

Heat, whether from fire or from a too ardently turned grindstone, endangers the temper of steel. A well tempered blade is a thing to cherish. Some lumberjacks will not leave an ax in green wood on the theory that this may draw the precious temper.

Safety

A sound way to avoid accidents with an ax is to work with a wide safety margin, sacrificing power and speed if need be for protection.

Experts handle an ax so that often the only safety margin is their supreme skill. Don't be an "expert." Be prepared to have the edge glance off a knot and be standing so that it will not matter. Make certain to clear away any brush that might deflect the blade, rather than to depend on the sure arc of the swing for insurance. Don't be one of the tribe who steadies a billet with hand

or foot. Try to foresee all possible mischances and to proceed so
that even if they should occur, no injury will result.

It has been pointed out that axes are far less dangerous than such
a very, very common substance as glass. Any shortcomings lie
not with the ax but with the individual.

Beaver Cutter

This is the disparaging term applied to the *munyasse* who severs
a log by hacking at it from all sides like a beaver who, despite
some opinion to the contrary, does not know where his timber
will topple.

It will save time if the notches are wide enough at the start.
When the log to be divided is on the ground, each of the two
notches necessary should be as wide as the diameter of the particular log at that point. Two such Vs, cut on opposite sides of the
log so that their points will meet at approximately its middle, will
separate the stick most economically.

Log Ends

Some builders prefer the picturesque appearance of the ax-cut
end on cabin logs. Wilderness residents to whom cabins are daily
matters generally settle for the neatly sawed extremity which is
somewhat more practical if only for the reason that it gathers less
moisture. The former has more individuality, a trait not without
favor if the axmanship is adept. It's all a matter of taste.

Squaring

Many pioneer structures, including the traditional Hudson's
Bay Company trading post, were made throughout of squared
timbers.

The only squaring demanded of most log cabin builders today,
however, is the flattening of an occasional surface such as those
portions of the sill logs which should rest solidly on the foundations.

Methods vary with workmen, but let it be noted that a log may
be flattened by walking along the top and scoring the side with
an easy swing of the ax—that is, making naturally slanting cuts
several inches apart to the approximate depth indicated by a

guide line. The chips are then hewn out by walking back the other way and cutting parallel along the guide line.

One can spend as much time as he wants from then on in slicing off a shaving here and another there until, if the workman has sufficient skill and patience, the surface can become as smooth as if it has been planed. A broadax properly used can simplify the task.

The inside walls of a cabin are sometimes hewn in this fashion, course by course as each is secured in place. This again is a mat-

Walk along log and with ax make slanting cuts to guide line

Then — walk back and cut parallel to guide line, hewing out chips

Hewing simplified.

ter of taste. A plumb interior of rounded logs is as functional for ordinary purposes as well hewn logs, and many prefer its appearance. Naturally rounded logs are certainly a whole lot more functional than poorly hewn ones whose splintery, unsightly, dust-gathering roughness remains a constant annoyance.

Various saws are used for squaring. They range from the crosscut to the heavy frame saw whose blade can be adjusted to different angles. Logs so sawed are generally first blocked on sawhorses or other supports at convenient heights.

Planes, drawshaves, and other such tools are all used for flattening logs. The rankest amateur can do a creditable job by sawing vertically at every six or so inches to a specified depth, then knocking out the blocks with mallet and chisel.

Pit Sawing

Thousands of massive planks have been turned out by pit sawing; one man wielding a long saw from a platform while a second man works below, perhaps in a pit depending on the elevation of the staging.

Pit sawing is said to have caused more enmities along the ever moving frontiers of the continent than any other occupation. The top man becomes certain that his partner is riding the saw on the upsweep. The latter soon feels as convinced that the other isn't doing much more than leaning on the downstroke.

Anyone who has ever dug sawdust out of his eyes and ears will testify that the choicer assignment is not the one looking up.

Lining

Logs are best squared to definite lines. It requires considerable skill to determine by eye alone when an edge is straight but little to handle measuring tape and chalk line.

A handy way to mark a straight line is by stretching a cord between two nails whose positions have been accurately measured, rubbing the cord liberally with chalk, and finally lifting it near the middle and letting it snap against the wood. Special cord and chalk are obtainable for a few cents.

Squaring by Horse

Horses are occasionally used if extensive squaring is to be done. One method is to set a weighty broadax blade in a plow-like frame. Logs may be laid on the ground in rough squares to save time. Vertical cuts are first sawed at every few feet along the logs to the depth desired. The workman then straddles a log and, horses hauling, plows the square.

A second method is to saw the vertical cuts as before, then to wedge each log in a trough at the depth so indicated and to pull a similar blade across it like a giant drawshave. The blade may be centered on a frame, each end of which is dragged by a horse walking on its respective side of the trough. The sides of this receptacle can be made to support the moving frame so that the blade will not cut too deeply.

The chips resulting from such work are sometimes used as shingles.

Splitting

Most logs are readily split if the grain is true. This can be determined at a glance, after some experience, by looking to see that the log does not have many knots and that it has not twisted in its growth.

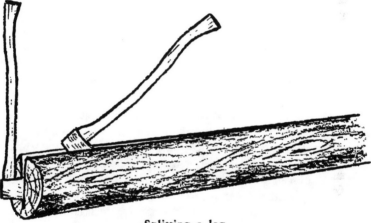

Splitting a log.

When one has two axes, not even wedges are required for splitting. The crack is started by burying an ax in the center of the butt. The second ax, driven into the butt near the top, widens the fracture and frees the first ax. A line is followed across the top with first one ax and then the other.

If one is uncertain of his axmanship, two wedges and a sledge hammer will do the trick.

Sawing Guides

When logs with square ends are called for, it will be well to use some sort of a guide to direct the saw. This may be two square-

Guide for sawing straight ends.

ended planks nailed together in a wide V that can be inverted across each log to conduct the blade.

It is frequently necessary to prepare a number of logs of equal length. Then it will often save time to build a contrivance of sorts to regulate the cutting. Possibilities are limited by little except ingeniousness and materials at hand.

One elementary arrangement is a long receptacle, open at both ends, made of three planks nailed together at right angles. Let's assume that a cabin eighteen feet long and twelve feet wide is to be built with corner posts taking the place of notches. The trough is then made eighteen feet long. Pains are taken to fashion each end exactly square. Then a log can be slid into the holder and, once moved so that its best portion will be utilized, sawed swiftly to measure with each end of the trough guiding the blade.

A carefully measured and squared twelve feet from one end

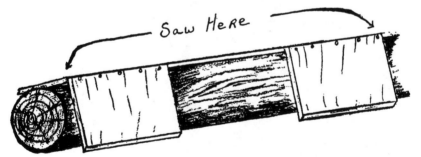

A handy variation of the mitre-box principle.

of this same trough, a saw cut may be made that will direct the blade in the manufacture of the shorter logs. Numerous other improvisions of this mitre-box principle can be figured out to fit the job at hand.

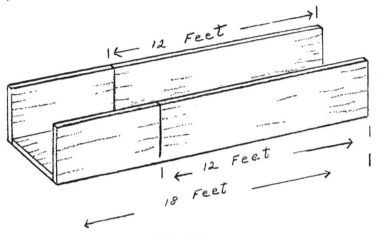

Mitre Box.

Mitre Box

A mitre box can be made in a few minutes with three pieces of board or plank, as shown by the drawing. It may be two or three feet long. It should be wide enough to accommodate whatever sticks the builder will need to insert in it.

The two longer edges of the mitre box's base must be straight and parallel. After the two sides have been nailed on, a straight line should be drawn across the bottom at right angles with the aid of a try square and then followed up and across each side. A saw cut should then be carefully made down through both sides to the base. When a stick is held tightly against one of the sides, this slit will guide the saw in cutting a square end.

The mitre box will similarly act as a guide for cuts made at other specified angles. The bevel may be cut in the sides of the box with, for example, a sample rafter being used as the guide. Then all other rafters can be easily sawed to that standard which

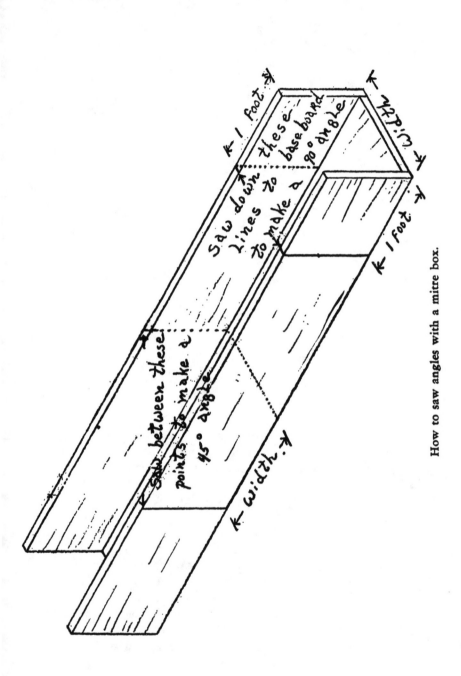

How to saw angles with a mitre box.

48

in cabin work will be the important thing. It will make no difference if the roof of the log house has a forty-two instead of a forty-five per cent pitch, in other words, so long as the same angle is followed throughout.

It is easy enough incidentally, as shown in the drawing, to make a slit in the mitre box that will guide the saw on an exact forty-five degree angle. A distance equal to the width of the box is measured along one bottom side. With the help of try square, a vertical line should then be drawn from one end of this measurement up to the outer top of one side. A similar vertical line should extend from the other end to the outside top of the opposite side. A saw cut connecting these two points will form a guide for the sawing of a forty-five degree angle.

Sawhorse

The simplest sawhorse is two poles driven into the ground to form an X. A chunk of wood jammed between the lower gap in this contrivance will steady it. The X is often wired together in the middle for further support. Two such sawhorses placed conveniently side by side will save a lot of maneuvering and stooping.

Labor Saver

A handy portable sawhorse is made by cutting a hole in two heavy slabs, their flat sides crossed and spiked, and inserting a long pole which is nailed in place.

Canny individualists sometimes improve this labor-saver by boring holes at frequent intervals along the top of the pole. A ponderous log may then be levered up the gradually slanting incline with a minimum of effort and held, whenever a breathing spell is desired, by a peg inserted behind it at easy stages.

Some Considerations

A living barrier of trees is nature's protection from storm and boisterous wind. Dead or threatening growth should be removed before construction is commenced. Some towering trees such as poplars and cottonwoods, whose lower branches die as energy is concentrated on climbing toward the sun, are prime offenders in the matter of unexpectedly tumbling limbs.

Fuel

A lasting supply of firewood, unless some other fuel is to be used, is a more important consideration for the permanent camp than nearby building logs. When the latter have been brought to the site the matter is ended. Woodpile replenishing is an endless task.

Native wood piles will usually furnish information as to the best available local fuels. Shellback hickory leads the North American woods in heat producing power, followed in order by pignut hickory, white oak, white ash, dogwood, scrub oak, apple tree, red oak, white beech, yellow oak, hard maple, white elm, red cedar, wild cherry, yellow pine, chestnut, yellow poplar, butternut, white birch, and white pine. The last is regarded as less than one-third as efficacious as either hickory.

Hardwoods in general give comparatively steady fires and lasting coals. The resinous softwoods, habitually noisy and short lived, make excellent kindling. Pine, often standing, fire-killed stuff, is nevertheless the principal fuel of many a backwoods community.

Ringing

A trapper's dodge to assure a dry supply of winter wood is to "ring" a number of standing trees before quitting his line in the spring. This he does by chopping into the trunk all the way around. The sticks, their sap prevented from rising, die on the stump and are ready for later cutting.

Some trees burn better when green. Split live birch makes a hot steady blaze except in very cold weather. Then the frozen chunks retard the fire until kindling temperature is reached.

Pine Slivers

Long pine slivers, placed conveniently near stove or fireplace, will help to conserve matches as they did in bygone days.

"Every man looks at his woodpile with a kind of affection," Thoreau noted. "I loved to have mine before my window, and the more chips the better to remind ¡me of my pleasing work. How much more interesting an event is that man's supper who has just been forth in the snow to hunt the fuel to cook it with!"

CHAPTER FIVE

FOUNDATION DEPARTMENT

"If you have built castles in the air, your work need not be lost," Thoreau found when he took to the woods a century ago. "That is where they should be. Now put the foundations under them." The site has been selected. Logs are straight and sound. Stakes mark where the wilderness home is to rise. Pioneer women in olden days would be preparing a feast for neighbors due to congregate for the log-raising bee.

Cornerstones

The cabin foundation may be as simple as one desires, but it should be solid and level throughout if work is not to be unnecessarily prolonged.

Four cornerstones, embedded with flat surfaces upraised, will suffice in dry climates if the ground is firm and the structure small. None need be larger than what one man can move easily.

Pits filled with rocks can be improvised as bases for these supports in locations where the earth is soft.

Two flat stones at each corner are greatly preferable. Moisture climbs single stones and rots woodwork. But if one slab is laid atop another above the ground and not cemented, dampness will be barred by the juncture from rising by capillary attraction to decay the sills.

Support

Log cabins should be supported at the corners and at about every six feet. A cabin approximately twelve feet wide and eighteen feet long, to give a common example, needs an additional bolster at the middle of each short span. Two more props should be spaced equidistant beneath each long sill.

Height

Cabins, by their very nature, best hug the warm, shielding earth from which the logs themselves have sprung. Many a cabin wall rises from the wilderness floor itself. This is successful only in dry country, however. Then it is generally inadvisable except for temporary structures.

Cabins partially subterranean are not uncommon among trappers and prospectors in regions where the ground is frozen the year around a short distance below the surface. This practice saves heat, materials, and labor for these sons of the silent places.

It is particularly advisable in humid zones (and sound practice almost anywhere) for all wood in the wilderness home to be at least ten inches above the ground at the nearest point. Climate is the prime determinant. One observes cabins set directly on the soil in the semi-arid interiors of the Yukon and British Columbia that are sound after two decades or more. Yet I've seen a cabin built with dirt sills beside the salmon-silvered Grand Cascapedia River on Quebec's damp Gaspé Peninsula whose unpeeled bottom logs were crumbling with decay the second year.

Markers

A stake at each corner will do to mark small cabins with simple foundations, inasmuch as leveling and squaring will be accomplished by the trial and error method, anyway. The tapering nature of logs makes work with them more a matter of approximation and compromise than of precise measuring, such as is possible with lumber.

It is obvious that a marker set directly at a corner will have to be moved when any sort of foundation is put there. When one goes beyond the plainest form of base, he can save time by em-

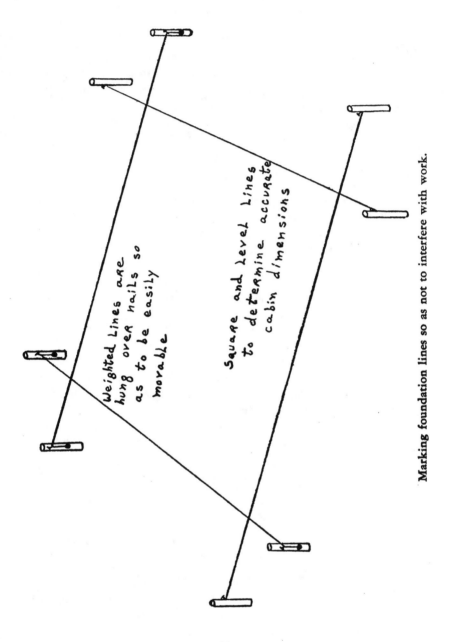

Weighted lines are hung over nails so as to be easily movable

Square and level lines to determine accurate cabin dimensions

Marking foundation lines so as not to interfere with work.

54

ploying a method that will indicate levels and angles at all times. Accurate enough for ordinary log cabin purposes is the simple extension of each foundation line. This can be done by driving an additional stake some five feet beyond it at each end in a straight line.

Approximate levels are marked by a nail slanted into the side of each of the eight stakes. Weighted lines laid across these nails will intersect to indicate foundation corners.

The corners are then trued with the aid of a carpenter's square or any other right angle, a square-edged board perhaps or the cover of this book. Whenever any two diagonally opposite corners are adjudged to be right angles, the entire rectangle will be proved square.

Then one starts at the corner nearest the ground, sets it at the desired height, and brings the four sides in turn to that common level. Use of a regular level, or even a long slim water-filled bottle in which an air bubble can be centered, will make this task simple.

A Level

Numerous manufactured levels are sold. There is no need for the cabin builder to purchase an expensive elaborate type, inasmuch as all that is needed is a straight-edged frame in which two fluid-filled transparent tubes are set, one horizontally and another vertically. The air bubble in each finds the clearly marked center of its respective container when the surface against which the straight edge is held is level or plumb as the case may be.

When the surface being tested is out of line, tilting the level's straight edge until the proper bubble becomes centered will show how much of an adjustment should be made.

Foundation Posts

Wooden foundation posts are best set at least three feet deep in rock-bottomed pits. A single slab embedded solidly at the base of each excavation with its flat surface upraised will provide a sufficient base in firm ground. Added insurance, advisable in soft footing, can be had by dropping additional rocks around the post as the hole is filled.

Only durable woods such as cedar, juniper, redwood, locust,

cypress, chestnut, osage orange, and iron oak should be used. If other species must be employed, they should be liberally treated with creosote or one of the other preservatives on the market. Such precautions will not be amiss with even the more rugged woods.

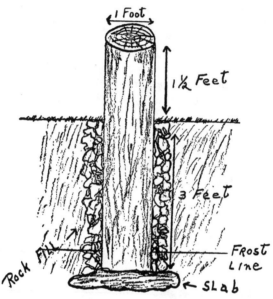

Wooden foundation post.

Wooden posts should be at least one foot in diameter. Any portions of their tops that are not eventually covered by the construction should be cut at a slant so that water will not collect there to seep into the wood along its natural grain. Any protective coating of creosote thus disturbed should be renewed.

Wooden foundation posts at best are not in the same class with rock or concrete supports.

Creosote

Creosote is useful in offering all vulnerable parts of the wilderness home a certain amount of protection from decay-inducing dampness and from insect ravages. It has one advantage over some other preservatives in that it can be easily, quickly, effectively, and inexpensively applied by hand.

The creosote used for foundation work may be the regular thick, blackish coal tar product inasmuch as there probably will be no objection to staining the posts. The builder who would like to retain the natural color of the wood as much as possible can use first grade, liquid oil, coal tar creosote on those portions appearing above ground.

The creosote can be easily and safely heated by placing the open container in a wide pan of water which is then brought to a boil. This procedure will prevent the creosote from spilling over and igniting.

The hot creosote should be thickly and thoroughly brushed over every portion of the peeled dry post. When the initial coat has dried, a second should be applied. The post should thereafter be handled with reasonable care. Any damage to the protective coating should be repaired with additional creosote before the support is finally embedded.

The applicator used with creosote may be a brush manufactured particularly for that work, a paint brush whose bristles have been stiffened by windings of wire, or a soft, old broom.

Termites

Several local inquiries will usually warn the prospective builder what he should guard against in the way of destructive insects. Usually no special precautions whatsoever will have to be taken. Beetles occasionally may be a pest in a particular section, and then one of the simple steps enumerated in Chapter Three will provide an easy solution.

If termites may be neighbors, no-trespassing signs can be put out against them without too much effort. A naturally resistant wood such as cypress or redwood will help solve the problem. Creosote is a deterrent. Its thorough application to all wood nearer than eighteen inches to the ground is counseled. Logs and floors, in fact, are best kept at least that high at all points.

Portland cement should be used for any concrete or masonry foundations, and this work should be kept solid throughout so as not to provide any tunnels for the so-called "white ants."

Metal termite guards are installed easily and cheaply, but if other less drastic precautions are heeded when there may be termite trouble, these barriers are seldom necessary. The termite guard is merely a shield of galvanized iron, copper, zinc, or other rust-resistant metal. It should cover the entire top of the wooden foundation and, projecting some four inches all around, should then be bent downward at about a forty-five degree angle. With

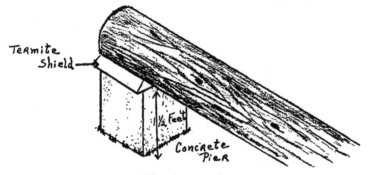

Termite guard.

solid masonry or concrete foundations, metal strips six inches or so wide may be inserted in the mortar on each side of the top and then bent downward on a forty-five degree slant—that is, half way between horizontal and vertical.

If there should be any pipes reaching from cabin to ground, these should be tightly ringed with shields which may either be purchased or cut and bent in a moment from sheet metal.

Prospectors building on corner posts sometimes invert a picturesque old gold pan over the top of each prop and, rightly satisfied, call it a day.

Piers

Concrete piers may be cast at each corner in rock bottomed pits that extend well below frost level. These pits should be at least three feet deep unless bed rock is encountered first. The work can be eased by the use of crude wooden forms, tapering from tops eight to twelve inches square to somewhat larger bases. When the poured concrete has set, the form may be taken off and used for the next pier. Daubing its inside with grease or soap will make removal easier.

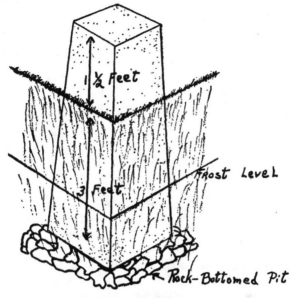

Concrete pier.

The concrete can be made to provide its own base by pulling up the form about a foot and letting the poured concrete spread across the bottom of the excavation which in this case should be about two-feet square.

When particularly high piers are to be made, lumber and time may be saved in firm ground by digging a hole about two-feet square to the desired depth and pouring the concrete directly into that. As soon as the hole is nearly filled, the form may then be set in place for the remaining distance.

Forms

All temporary wooden forms used for such work should be lightly nailed so that they can be easily knocked apart. A two-headed nail, whose first head holds the board firmly in place and whose second head remains extended, is manufactured for this purpose.

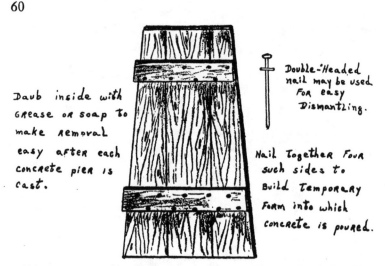

Daub inside with Grease or soap to make removal easy after each concrete pier is cast.

Double-Headed nail may be used for easy Dismantling.

Nail Together Four such sides to Build Temporary Form into which concrete is poured.

Temporary wooden forms for piers. Use of a two-headed nail.

It will save effort if pains are taken to make the top of the form straight. The form may then be set with the aid of the level so that the top of the concrete, smoothed by a board drawn across the form, will end up painlessly horizontal.

Concrete

Concrete for use in wilderness home foundations may well consist of one part of Portland cement by volume, two parts of clean coarse sand, and four parts of large screened gravel or crushed rock.

Measurements, which need not be exact, can be made by the shovelful. All sand, gravel, and rock should be hard and free of dirt. Small particles should be screened out of the gravel and crushed stone which, unless it is clean, should be hosed or otherwise washed. An aggregrate that will pass through a screen with openings two inches square will be satisfactory.

One part of Portland cement by volume can also be used with six parts of clean unscreened gravel which varies in size from very coarse sand to pebbles.

Inasmuch as materials differ considerably, particularly in the wilderness, the soundest procedure is to mix several small test batches and to change the proportions methodically in each. After the test mixtures have been allowed to set and cure for a week, the builder will be able to judge what combination to use.

The experimenter will take into account that the toughness and solidity of cement is determined by the percentages of cement, water, and sand therein. No more water should be added therefore than is needed to make a thick, thoroughly moistened substance that will flow sufficiently to seek its own level. The more one mixes concrete after it has been moistened, the smoother and stauncher it will be. It should be used a half-hour after the first water has been added, however.

Gravel and crushed stone are used only as fillers. When foundation or similar work is being done, the concrete can be safely stretched by embedding clean wet rocks throughout. Care should be taken that these fillers are substantially surrounded on every side by tightly packed concrete. One should work along the side of the form with a spade or stick to keep gravel or crushed rock from massing near the surface.

Finishing

A cement less coarse than that required for mass work is often desired for finishing concrete steps, occasional floors of outbuildings, and other such surfaces.

A satisfactory formula for this purpose is one part Portland cement by volume to three parts of clean sand. Fine sand will allow a smoother finish than will coarse. Only the final inch needs to be made of this material. It should be added before the mass cement has hardened and then spread with a trowel until enough water is smoothed to the surface to reveal an apparently mirror-like glaze.

When sand is not available, as minute, clean gravel as can be found can be substituted in the same ratio.

Rusticity

Concrete piers may be camouflaged with vines, shrubs, bark fastened by wire, or by paint. Commercial colors mixed with the cement are also used. Five pounds of chromium oxide per bag of cement will yield a forest green. Three or four pounds of burnt umber will result in a quiet brown. Five pounds of yellow ochre will give a yellow.

Mortar Box

It will save time and materials to build a mortar box if any sizable amount of concrete or mortar is to be mixed. Such a box can be utilized later for compounding chinking for the cabin walls.

The main requirement is that the mortar box be as watertight as possible, inasmuch as any fluid running from it while the mixing is going on will be enervating the artificial stone by wasting cement.

The mortar box may be built of wood. No particular dimensions are called for, although a contraption two yards long and one yard wide will be a handy size for the cabin builder. The sides may be about eight inches high. Outwardly slanting ends are convenient. The seams can be tightened by sinking the box in water so that the wood seams will swell shut.

Gravel or crushed rock, sand, and cement are shoveled or hoed while dry, until an evenness of color indicates that they are very thoroughly blended. Water is then added gradually bit by bit, and the mixing continued as long as feasible. Cement should be used within a half-hour after the water has been added, if I may repeat. Trying to extend this limit by putting in more water will only weaken the compound.

Reinforced Concrete

Concrete piers can be strengthened considerably be reinforcing them with about a half-inch iron rod some three inches from each corner. These rods should be tied together at one-foot intervals with heavy wire.

A reinforcement of heavy wire fencing, not less than eleven gauge, will guard a concrete slab against cracking.

Mortar And Masonry

Mortar is the substance used to join stones and bricks. The result is masonry.

Mortar for amateur use should not be proportionately leaner than one 94-pound bag of Portland cement, nine pounds of hydrated lime, and three times this combined volume of coarse, clean sand.

All dry mixtures should be stirred and shoveled until a constancy of color signifies that they are well mingled. Only enough water should then be gradually added to make a smoothly flowing paste that is firm enough when wet to support whatever masonry is being laid up.

All stones and all previously completed masonry should be well dampened before fresh mortar is troweled into place. In cold weather, both should be dry and, whenever practicable, warm. Stones should be well bedded in mortar and thus prevented from touching any other stone. No joints between stones should extend vertically for more than one tier.

Lime Mortar

Lime mortar may be utilized for foundation work, although it is now considered generally inadvisable to employ anything less than a rich cement mortar for fireplace work. Lime mortar is mixed in the ratio of four parts of sand by volume to one part of lime.

"I worked so deliberately," wrote Thoreau when he used it for a chimney, "that though I commenced at the ground in the morning, a course a few inches above the floor served for my pillow at night. Yet I did not get a stiff neck for it that I remember. My stiff neck is of older date."

Masonry Piers

Both masonry and reinforced concrete piers are stronger than ordinary concrete supports. Preparations for a masonry pier are commenced by digging a hole some two feet square. Unless bed rock is reached first, this should either be three feet down or more, if a greater depth is necessary to bring it well below the frost line.

The excavation is most easily filled in many localities with large rocks set as solidly as possible and then bound with mortar that is flowed around them. This base can be topped above the surface with regular masonry.

Masonry Walls

These are sometimes used for log cabins, especially when sandstone is available in flat uniform sections that speed the work.

All parts of the wall that actually support the cabin should be based on stone, concrete, or masonry foundations below the frost level. Such foundations should be about twice as broad as the supporting wall which may range from eight to twelve inches in thickness.

Portions of the wall that do not bear weight, but which are actually fillers, need not be so based. A narrow clearance should be left between them and the bottom logs in such cases, however, so that if they are heaved upward by the freezing earth they will not disturb the sills.

Air should be allowed to circulate freely beneath the floor during temperate weather so that wood-rotting dampness will not attack floors and sills. Rectangular openings, therefore, may well be framed in at least two opposite sides of a foundation wall, screened across their interiors, and provided with easily closed wooden panels at the outsides so as to serve both as ventilators and storage spaces.

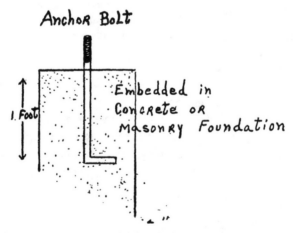

Anchor bolt.

Bolts

A long bolt may be embedded in the concrete or masonry at each corner to anchor the sill logs. Holes are subsequently burned through these sticks with a hot iron, or better drilled by brace and bit, and the log tightened to the foundation with a washer and nut on top, countersunk.

Frost Line

Freezing temperatures reach down into the very earth, turning the moisture therein to ice and thereby causing it to expand. Depths which cold reaches and heaves vary so greatly that the frost level of the particular section where the wilderness home is to be built should be ascertained locally.

Foundations that are at all elaborate should be based either safely below the frost line or on bed rock. When simple foundations consisting of single or double stones are used to support small log cabins, however, only mild attention is paid frost in dry terrain. Care is taken that the ground is not frozen where the stones are placed, so that it will not later sink and drop the foundation out of line. Bushmen who happen to be building in cold weather, therefore, find it a good idea to build rousing bonfires at the points where corner stones are to be set.

Sills

The sill logs are the wall logs that rest directly on the cabin foundations. They should be surpassed in strength and straightness, therefore, only by the ridgepole. If one is building mainly with green stock, it will be wise to locate sound standing deadwood for these key sticks whenever possible.

The sill logs should be based as solidly as possible on the foundations. It is frequently best to square them at points of contact for this reason. This may be done by saw, chisel and mallet, plane, adz, or even ax as explained in the previous chapter. The bottom logs along the two longer sides are often the only true sills. When this is the case, the two shorter logs of the initial rectangle will lie about a half-log higher when they have been notched into

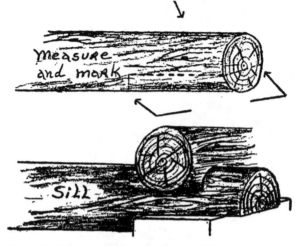

Two sills. Logs can be easily flattened by two saw cuts.

place. They may be firmly joined by either the saddle notch or the tenon joint, explained among others in the next chapter.

Four Sills

With certain types of corners, all four of the basic wall logs will be sills. All, that is, will then lie directly on the foundations and will support the walls.

Junctures in this case are easily and strongly made by half laps. To start with, all four logs should have approximately the same average diameter. Care should be taken that each pair, the longer two and the shorter two, should respectively be of equal lengths.

The joints may be prepared by cutting from the end of each log a chunk that is half that particular log's depth and that is as long as the total width of the log end to be joined to it. The accompanying drawing shows how simple the whole procedure is. A total of sixteen saw cuts, eight vertical and eight horizontal, are all that's needed.

Splicing

Logs occasionally have to be spliced to gain length, although the procedure should be avoided whenever possible. The sim-

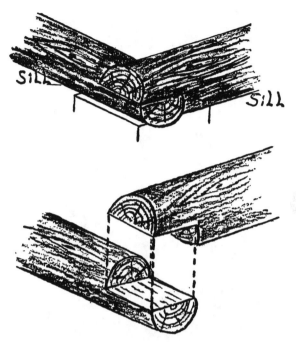

Four sills.

plest lap joint is also the one most preferable when splicing does have to be done. This is made by cutting a half section some three feet long from an end of each stick, and spiking the juncture.

Ingenuity

The North American log cabin traditionally is a wilderness home built with whatever tools may be at hand. The pioneers who hewed two great countries out of the unspoiled places north of the Rio Grande put up thousands by ax alone.

Modern frontiersmen, among whom ax work is becoming a lost art, are doing neater, although not always rapid, work with saws and hammers.

Where tools are few, ingenuity flourishes. The square, even if it be but the upper back corner of an ax head, should be kept busy. The measuring implement, steel tape or primitive notched stick, should be worked overtime.

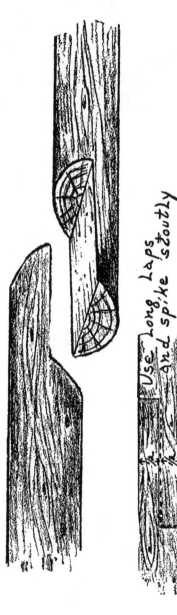

Use long laps and spike stoutly

How logs are cut for splicing.

A nail, a soft-nosed cartridge, or the burned end of a stick can replace the carpenter's pencil. Any of these tied to a thong will make a compass. The butt of an ax that has been driven into a stump becomes a backwoods anvil.

The builder not wishing to imitate that ever further tilting Leaning Tower of Pisa needs no expensive level. The bushmen's plate of water will do. The contrasting color of tea or coffee will make this device even more satisfactory, while the long slim bottle of fluid with its telltale air bubble is perfection too fine for any but the very good.

CHAPTER SIX

NOTCHES OR NOT

"Every child begins the world again," Thoreau noted. "It plays house, having an instinct for it. Who does not remember the interest with which, when young, he looked at any approach to a cave? It was the natural yearning of that portion of our most primitive ancestor which still survived in us."

Log Walls

Log walls, which generally can be put up in one or two weeks, are complete in themselves. The builder does not have to bother with studs, shoes, girts, braces, and a dozen other complications.

When the walls are caulked and chinked, which as later explained can usually be accomplished within two days at no expense other than perhaps the cost of some nails, all insulating and weatherproofing will be finished.

So, in most cases, will all necessary interior decorating. Painting, plastering, paneling, or papering a fresh bright log wall is about as effective as desecrating a fine old flintlock—or a lily—with gilt.

Fitting

Log cabin walls traditionally are not supposed to bear any resemblance to cabinet work. They should boast, instead, a rugged boldness. Fine and fancy log fittings are better reserved for costly lodges and for expensive city dwellings than imitated by the builder of the wilderness home.

Many think log cabin building is a whole lot more difficult than it really is. A major reason for this error is that fanciful walls are visualized that fit with scarcely a crack. The opposite condition is more often true. This is as it should be. The spaces are valuable in that their variability permit the easy leveling and truing of the structure.

The experienced log cabin builder therefore generally values crannies and crevices for the assets they can be. He realizes what a simple and effective matter it will be to close them later with moss and with clay mortar, for instance, both free for the using. He therefore knows he need not worry about the spaces between logs except to limit them whenever possible to a maximum of some two inches.

Plumb

Log walls should be kept reasonably plumb along their interiors. They should run as straight up and down as possible, that is.

No harm is done if the inside walls are not vertical along their outer contours. It's just easier to install cabinets and to arrange furniture, that's all, if one log bulges no further into the room than another.

It takes considerable skill to keep a wall in line by eye alone. Only patience and a certain amount of common sense are required if one has the assistance of a plumb line or a level.

A plumb line is merely a string to one end of which is affixed a weight, called a bob, particularly when one discusses possible purchase. A plumb line adequate for log work can be made by knotting a piece of twine around a sinker or a cartridge. When this weighted cord is suspended free, gravity will of course straighten it into a perfectly vertical guide line.

Successive logs can also be quickly plumbed, then marked, with the assistance of a level and a straight edge. The latter, usually a board, is laid against the interior wall to guide the inner bulge of each new log into place. When a carpenter's level is held lengthwise against the board, the centering of the air bubble in the then horizontal tube at the end will indicate when the wall is plumb.

The appearance of the cabin interior will be improved if some

Interior walls should be kept vertical.

care is taken to turn the most presentable side of each log inward whenever possible. If the wall log has a pronounced bend, however, it may prove more desirable to face the concave side inward in any case.

Level

The tapering nature of logs makes work with them a matter of compromise and approximation rather than precise measuring, such as is possible with milled lumber.

The less the logs taper, the easier the work will be. It is even possible in some sections of this continent to find trees growing so tall and thick that cabin logs can be cut that will vary scarcely an inch or two in circumference from top to bottom.

Taper can be made to balance itself so that rising walls can be kept reasonably level. Each log butt will contact a log top at every corner. Each tier, in other words, will run in an opposite direction from any directly above and any directly below. Walls will keep themselves reasonably level, that is, if one course of reasonably uniform sticks is layed clockwise butt to top, butt to top, butt to top, and butt to top—and the next layer is put down top to butt, top to butt, top to butt, and top to butt; and so on.

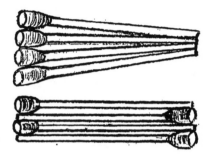

Compensating for the natural taper in logs.

An easy way to visualize what happens is by experimenting with four long wooden matches. Press them together in a tight flat rectangle with the unlighted heads all at the same end. The match heads, wider as the log butts are wider, will produce a fan effect. Then move the first and third matches so that the heads face the opposite direction. Note how a comparatively even rectangle is formed.

Bends

Some builders occasionally saw a log partially through so that a bend will flatten out under the pressure of the wall. This practice, like splicing, should be avoided whenever possible.

Corners

The foundations are true. The wall logs are in two convenient piles. The sills, those logs resting directly on the foundations, have been readied according to the directions in Chapter Five.

What type of corner is going to be used to hold the wall logs in place? There is plenty of room for choice. No set rules govern any part of log cabin construction. Log cabin builders often with ingenuity and sometimes with just plain orneriness, have historically followed a single axiom although they have expressed it in many different ways—the best you can, with what you have, right now!

Corner Posts

The quickest and easiest way to build log cabin walls is by spiking sawed logs directly between corner posts. This method is also the most economical one; insofar as getting the largest cabin possible for the logs used is concerned. The full length of each stick is utilized. None is lost by lapping or notching, techniques

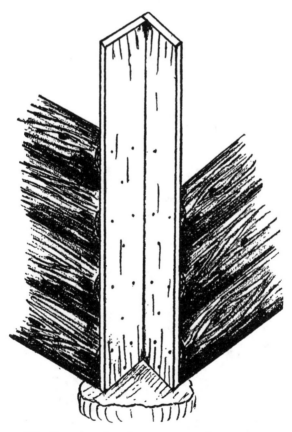

The fastest and easiest way to make corners.

that usually require each log to be several feet longer for a cabin of identical size.

When milled stock is available, a simple way to prepare the frames for square corners is by nailing two planks together at right angles. Four sets should be made, each a safe few inches

Reinforcing log, made by flattening two sides of small log, can be spiked in at conclusion. Round poles are often used. Logs can be spiked directly to corner posts, too.

taller than the walls will probably rise, inasmuch as it will be easier to trim than to lengthen them.

Posts to reinforce these frames can be made by flattening two sides of small logs until each resembles an elongated quarter of pie. One of these can be later spiked into the open angle at each corner for reinforcement. A round pole may be similarly installed, of course. Poles hewn into quarter-pie shape are often used by themselves for corner posts.

The stoutest way to start the square corner is by spiking each support vertically to a rugged base of four sill logs. An easier way to begin the square corner is by setting the supports on the cabin foundations themselves, then laying the four sill logs between them.

A compromise, incorporating both motifs, finds the shorter sill logs spiked across the ends of the longer sills. One of each right-angled pair of planks is left the width of a sill log longer than its fellow and is held in the juncture.

The wall logs are sawed to measure on the ground, rolled into position between the corner supports, and each spiked at least twice at each end. One fastener alone too often becomes a pivot on which the stick will roll.

It will usually save time to prepare these logs in quantity, using one of the several contrivances mentioned in Chapter Four to assure their having square ends and standard lengths.

Fastening

The advantages of the square corner are offset, to some extent, by one shortcoming. This is its proportional instability when compared to the solidity of the notched corners. This weakness can be largely removed if the logs are pegged or spiked to one another every three or four feet.

The practice of fastening wall logs together is a sound one for the cabin builder to follow, no matter what type of corner he adopts.

Spikes may be used. If those available are not long enough to grip the second log securely, the upper stick can be bored with brace and bit or auger and the spikes countersunk in the cavities thus provided. Use of a blacksmith's hammer or even a sledge will speed this latter task. When the head of the spike is driven to the level of the top log, a short iron bar may be used with the hammer, as a countersink, to force it to the full depth of the depression. This bar should be just a fraction smaller than the hole.

Dowels

True Scottish frugality is said to have resulted in not a nail's being used in the original houses of Fort Victoria, former stockaded Hudson's Bay Company trading post, now the capital of British Columbia. Wooden pegs were cheaper.

Dowels have their place in even the most modern wilderness home. To substitute them for spikes in reinforcing a wall, one has only to bore a hole through one log and part way in the next at intervals of about four feet and to hammer in substantial pegs. All boring should be staggered, tier for tier, so as not to interfere with holes drilled in preceding logs.

Softwood pegs will adapt themselves without careful whittling. Oaken and similar hardwood varieties will have to be more precisely fashioned.

Rough Square

This type of corner is sometimes chosen by the axman doing rough, quick work without a saw. Corner posts, either squared in quarter-pie fashion or left round, are spiked inside the four sill logs. Wall logs, usually unpeeled, are then rapidly laid up and spiked against—not between—these supports.

No log ends need be square as is necessary with the previously described corner. The logs do not even have to be of regular lengths so long as they will reach between posts. One end of each is kept even with the post by the protruding extremities of one adjoining wall. The other end is not restricted in any way, although it may later be trimmed.

Except in cases of emergency or temporariness, this type of construction has little to recommend it except the ease and the speed with which it can be completed. Once chinked, such a rough structure will be warm enough, however. Trappers, prospectors, and guides sometimes put up seldom used outlying buildings in this fashion.

Rough square corner. Fast ax-work for temporary structures.

Notches

The position and width of notches are determined by rolling each wall log into place and then marking on it—and on the log below in the case of interlocking notches—the width of the contacting log where they are to be joined.

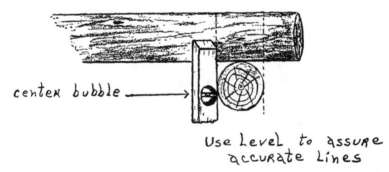

Marking position and width of notches. The use of level to assure accurate lines.

This sounds a whole lot more complicated than it really is, as a glance at the following drawings of the more common notches will indicate. There is nothing difficult or complex about log work. If there had been, the largely unskilled men who with a minimum of tools and a maximum of haste dotted this continent with widely flung log cabins would have turned to some other method of building.

No ax is needed for notching a log. They may be sawed, gouged, chiseled, or even whittled into shape. The job isn't limited to fictional experts who take a quick Hollywood squint, nod, and then proceed to hew a flawless joint with a few swift strokes. In real life, one measures and marks where the joint is to go, then follows the guide lines.

Saddle Notch

The saddle notch is a favorite, particularly in damp climates, because no niche is left upturned to gather moisture.

The two sill logs are in place. Now one of the shorter end logs is rolled into position. Its butt rests on the top of one sill log, and in turn its top angles across the butt of the other sill. The end log

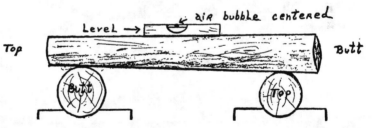

Roll one of end logs in position across sills to start saddle notch.

is now shifted until its straightest length lies horizontally. The more presentable of the other two sides is turned inward to give the inner wall the best possible appearance. If there is much bend to the log, however, the convex side is turned outward to keep the inner wall more plumb.

The level is laid along the top of the log. Let's assume that the telltale bubble lingers at the center of the horizontal tube, showing that the log is already level. The two notches, therefore, need to be half the respective thickness of each end of the log. Each notch will be as wide, of course, as that portion of the sill logs each will cover.

Each saddle notch will be ideally half as deep as its log is thick.

One end of the short log is measured by a ruler laid through its center. It is, say, ten inches thick. The notch at that end will then be five inches deep. A compass such as one used in high school geometry may now be used, or some similar device may be improvised even if it's only a pencil held at the five-inch mark of the ruler.

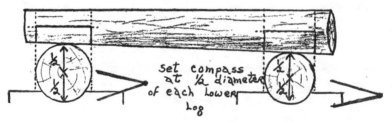

Compass may be used to mark exact curves.

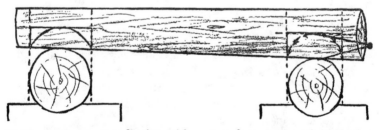

Hold compass perpendicular with one end on curve of lower log and mark on upper log the curve of the lower.

The compass, if that is utilized, is opened until the distance between metal top and pencil point measures the desired five inches. The metal tip is placed on the curve of the sill log and, the compass held perpendicular, it lightly follows the curve until a facsimile half circle is drawn on one side of the short log by the pencil. A similar mark is made on the other side of the short log.

Now the other end of the short log is measured. It proves to be twelve inches thick. The compass is opened to six inches and two similar arcs are drawn.

Each saddle notch will be as wide as the log each covers.

The short log is rolled over. The extreme width of each notch is indicated by connecting the respective bottom ends of each arc. Both notches are thereby plainly marked. All that remains is to cut them out. This may be done by ax, or it may be done by gouge. The nicks may be roughly sawed in triangular shape, then finished by sharp chisel and mallet. A saw cut may be made in the middle of the notch-to-be to the full depth and the notch hewn or gouged out in easy sections. Successive notches are so marked and so hollowed.

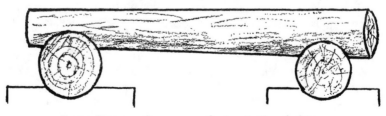

Succeeding notches are made in similar fashion.

Saddle notch corner.

Now let's assume that when the level was laid against the short log, the bubble showed that the stick was lower at one end than at the other. A small wedge, in that case, was driven further and further under the low end until the log proved level. Measuring then showed that the top of the log had to be lifted, say, one inch to make the log level. So instead of opening the compass five inches to measure that particular notch, the compass was narrowed the indicated one inch to four inches. A notch that deep, as one will understand after a little thought, will leave the log exactly level. The other notch, of course, will remain unchanged.

Technique

The walls will go up quicker and easier no matter what corner is used if, as succeeding tiers are raised, each log is so leveled that it is about two inches from the log beneath at the farthest point.

There is another school that prefers to touch up wall logs with an ax, plane, or other cutting tool so all meet in nearly straight lines. These techniques are discussed in Chapter Four. The most extreme of them is the squared log described in the same chapter.

Saddling

This method of fitting log walls is used seldom by bushmen but often by builders of lavish log lodges. It is practical only with the straightest, most thoroughly seasoned sticks. When skilfully done, it definitely pays off in functional beauty.

The lower side of each wall log is partially hollowed so that it will saddle the log beneath along its entire length. This cavity may be effected by ax alone or by such tools as a routing plane, adz, and gouge. A drawing compass will aid in figuring on the ends of the upper logs the curves of the lower. Connecting guide lines may then be marked along the two sides of each cupping log and the arduous hollowing and fitting process commenced.

Oakum or other long-lived caulking material should be placed within the saddling log to assure snugness.

Grooving

A modification of the saddling technique is to groove the underneath center of each closely fitting wall log, for its full length, just enough to hold and conceal the caulking.

Lock notch corner.

Lock Notch

This common notch is made by nicking both the upper and lower logs so that the sticks, when fitted, will lock one another in place. Instead of cupping the top of each lower log as in the case of the saddle notch, each lock notch curves into a similar hollow that is upraised on each lower log. The lock notch makes a stronger connection than does the saddle notch, but it is more vulnerable to dampness.

Hewn lock notches.

Hewn Lock Notch

Two particularly functional varieties of the lock notch can be made with square edges by saw, chisel and mallet, and of course by ax. Whereas round notches usually require more or less fitting, square notches can often be measured with sufficient preciseness to enable their being linked into place on the first try. The illustrations speak for themselves. The one with square edges is only slightly different from the tenon corner.

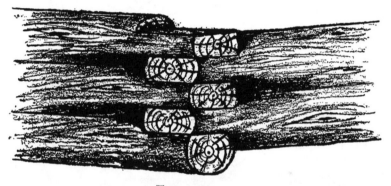

Tenon corner.

Tenon Corner

The tenon corner is the simplest example of how logs can be cut to fit over one another by saw alone. It is made by flattening the top and bottom extremities of each wall log so that the resulting tongues, each about half as wide as the diameter of the particular stick, will fit squarely upon one another.

The two long sills are squared and steadied into position. An end log is rolled into place, top over the butt of one sill and butt upon the top of the other sill. It is moved until the straightest length lies upright in the wall. The choicer of the other two sides is turned inward.

The next problem is to flatten the ends of both the wall log and the sills so that approximately half the former will extend above the sills. As in the explanation of the saddle notch, let's say that wall log lies level. If it doesn't, it's leveled the same way that other hypothetical log was.

Let's assume that the wall log has a diameter of twelve inches at the butt. That end, therefore, has to be dropped half this distance which is six inches. This is done by cutting three inches off the bottom end of the wall log and an equal amount off the top end of the particular sill.

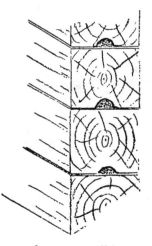

Snug caulking set in gouged grooves will insure tightness of squared-log walls.

Measurements should be made as carefully as possible. With the wall log held or blocked in the desired position, measure up the three inches from the bottom center of the butt. Measure down from the top center of the sill another three inches. With the aid of the level, draw straight and horizontal guide lines across the end of each log. Extend these lines along each side, as shown in the drawing.

It will be seen that each tongue can be made by one horizontal and one vertical cut. The saw may be used for both. Actually, the final appearance will be less rigid if only the horizontal cut is sawed and the slab is then freed by several strokes with an ax or hatchet.

Let's assume that the top of this same wall log has a diameter of ten inches. The top, then, will have to be lowered five inches. Half of this five inches will be taken in similar fashion from the wall log and the other half from that sill.

The uncut portions of the longer and shorter wall logs will be respectively the same throughout. For a cabin twenty feet long and twelve feet wide, that is, the side logs will run twenty feet in length between notches. The end logs will extend twelve feet between notches.

The length of the tongues will not matter, so long as they afford sufficient contact with adjoining logs to keep the wall steady. Actually, it will be both functional and pleasing to let the ends extend at varying lengths beyond the walls. Some builders, on the other hand, like to saw them off, when in place, so that all corners are square.

Each tongue, theoretically, is centered and is half as thick as the end of the log from which it is cut. If this is done throughout, however, all logs will either have to be perfectly straight to start

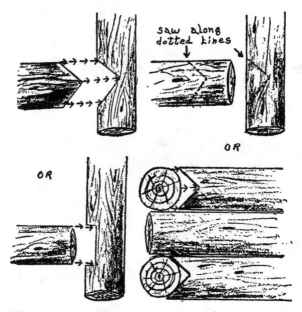

Side notches. Spike or peg corners and tiers strongly.

with or all irregularities will have to be smoothed off so that the logs will fit tightly.

What usually happens in actual construction is that the logs are measured and fitted so that distances of up to some two inches remain between the wall logs. This is accomplished by measuring so as to make the tongue slightly more than half as thick as its particular log. The discrepancy aids, too, in easily keeping the walls level.

Side Notch

Alternate ends of each log are butted into side notches by this method. Each log provides a side notch at one end, while the other end is fitted into a similar notch on the next log.

A dovetail corner.

Dovetailing

This technique is often chosen where a sawmill is handy to square seasoned logs to standard dimensions. Then all sticks can be made to conform on the ground with a prepared pattern.

If the diameters of the logs vary as they will when logs are round, each fitting will differ only in depth. All angles will remain the same.

In one favorite pattern in Alaska Highway country, the sides of otherwise round logs are flattened to a width of five inches for the last 20 inches. Tops and bottoms are left round up to the last six inches.

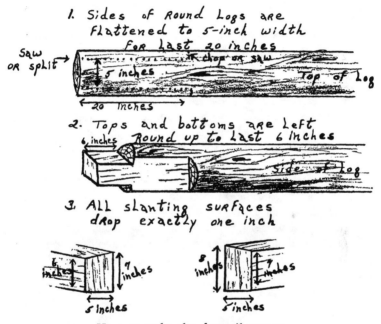

How to make the dovetail corner.

All slanting surfaces drop exactly one inch. If the taller measurement is seven inches, the slope is such that the shorter measurement is six inches. The illustration otherwise tells its own story.

HBC Corner

Traditional with the Hudson's Bay Company—to which, 2nd May 1670, Charles II of England gave a third of the North American continent—is the squared timber and mortised corner.

The mortised joint is effected by inserting tongued logs into substantial posts grooved by such tools as ax, chisel, gouge, adz, and plane.

Conventional round log construction has been comparatively unknown at Company posts except in British Columbia. Here, too, many a structure still stands that is built of short squared logs mortised at the corners and at intervals along the walls.

Choice

The builder need use only one type of corner. After reading this chapter and then selecting with some knowledge of the subject the corner he prefers, he may disregard the rest.

The detailed instructions given in this chapter embrace every fundamental of building log corners. One notched corner is shaped a little differently from another, but all are put together in the same general manner. All are measured, marked, and cut in similar fashion. Experiment with jackknife and four lengths of sapling, if you wish, until you have a practical working knowledge of how a saddle notch or a tenon corner is made and fitted. Then the detailed drawings of the other common corners will, after a little study, become self-explanatory.

You need have no misgivings. The log cabin, being characteristically low and rugged, requires no architectural perfection. Spikes and chinking will compensate for any technical shortcomings.

CHAPTER SEVEN

YOU DON'T HAVE TO BE HERCULES

Even Hercules might have had a time of it if forced to lift cabin logs into position by sheer strength. With some elementary knowledge, however, one or two boys can do the job with little exertion.

Block And Tackle

The easiest way to raise logs is with block and tackle. An adequate outfit can generally be borrowed in log cabin country without too much difficulty.

A rugged set may be purchased for a few dollars, on the other hand. It will pay in this extremity to buy at least one double block —which is two grooved pulleys set in a wooden or metal frame provided with a hook, preferably, for attaching it in a desired position. The other may be a single block, which contains but one sheave. Two doubles will ease the work, however. After the cabin is built, the block and tackle will continue to serve admirably for such tasks as hauling up boats and suspending big game.

The rope should be stout and strong, of course, but it need not be unduly large. A half-inch Manila line, for example, will be adequate for all ordinary work. Nylon ropes are stronger and longer lived, but some find them slippery to hold. A sisal line will do, but one should make sure of its tensile rating and secure one that's sufficiently husky.

The double block is attached to some stationary object, such as the cabin. A short piece of rope is looped several times around one

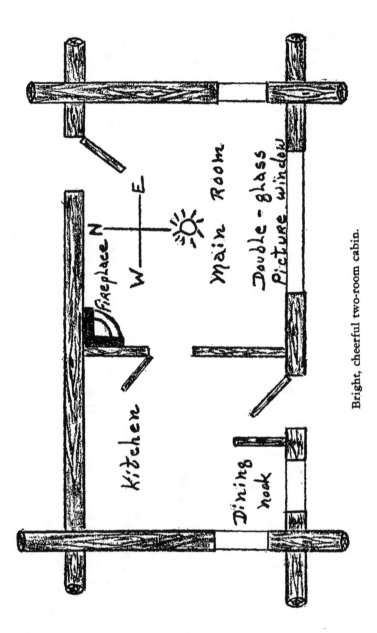

Bright, cheerful two-room cabin.

end of a log and then tied. The single block is then hooked to these loops.

One end of the long rope is now threaded permanently up and over the top pulley of the double block, down and over the grooved wheel of the single block, up and over the remaining pulley, and then back down to the single block where it is tied to the eye or whatever is provided there for the purpose. Use of two double blocks merely gears down the pull even more by use of a fourth pulley, after passing around which the end of the line is tied to the first block. Taking care not to twist and thereby bind the rope, the builder can haul away with an ease that will probably surprise him.

Tripod

The handiest way to use the block and tackle is with a crude tripod made by lashing the tops of three poles together. Such a tripod can be easily moved. The logs are lifted, one end at a time, by means of the block and tackle suspended from the top of this portable tower.

Skids

Two or more gradually slanting poles laid from ground to cabin wall serve as a skid up which, perhaps with the aid of ropes or with poles used as levers, logs can be readily moved. The usual procedure for the builder working alone is to raise one end of the log, secure it, and then lift the other end.

Pegged Skids

Particularly excellent for the builder working by himself is the pegged skid. This is made by boring holes every foot or so along two substantial poles. Pegs are then whittled and, as the log is gradually elevated end by end, are inserted behind it.

Ropes

Ropes are commonly used with skids to supplement or supplant levers. One method is to tie a pair behind the cabin wall, loop them down and around each end of the log to be lifted, and then to pass them back over the wall.

With one person hauling on each rope, the log will roll obedi-
ently up the incline. If no assistance is at hand, one end at a time
may be pulled up and lashed. The block and tackle will come in
particularly handy here. These same procedures can be accomplished without skids although not so easily.

Floors

The log cabin floor, for its own protection, is generally not
laid until the walls and roof have been completed. Its basic construction usually commences, however, as soon as the first course
of wall logs have been squared into position.

There is nothing laborious or difficult about flooring a log
cabin today. The job was always simple enough, but a deal of
work was involved when the wood had to be flattened by ax or
saw. That was and is one main excuse, in fact, for the tamped clay
or the just plain dirt floor which is warm, soft, noiseless, and certainly cheap, but whose advantages cease just about there.

Except for the expertly built and painstakingly oiled adobe
floor, preferably brightened with abundant protective rugs, the
dirt floor isn't one that the builder of a wilderness home will select if he has much choice in the matter.

An average sized cabin can usually be floored by one man in
one day if milled stock is used. This is a part of the cabin, as a matter of fact, where commercial lumber is ordinarily preferable to
rustic materials.

Stock Sizes

Whenever one plans to use any milled lumber in the construction of his wilderness home, it will be well to find out at the start
what lengths are available. This is particularly true in many remoter sections where supplies are not too complete. If the mill
only stocks flooring twelve-feet long and sixteen-feet long, for
example, one may as well think twice before putting up a cabin
that will require a fourteen-foot wide floor.

Joists

These horizontal beams running from wall to wall to support
the floor may as well be of milled materials since, hidden, they can

not detract from the rustic appearance of the log cabin. Man hours can thereby be saved that would otherwise be spent in flattening and in comparatively fussy fitting. The easiest way to base milled joists is on two-by-sixes spiked to the sill logs and preferably supported in addition by the foundation. Such joists, like all supporting timbers, are set with their narrower edges horizontal. They should be spiked to the sill logs as well as to the two-by-sixes.

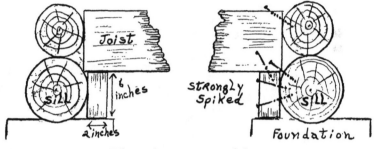

The easiest way to set joists.

The same procedure may be followed with poles. A smaller log is laid on the foundations on the inner side of the two long sill logs. Each pair is securely spiked together. Poles, which if sufficiently straight may be used without hewing except for any cuts necessary at either end to make them lie at a common level, are then spiked into place for joists.

Projecting Ends

Another method is to lay the joists in grooves cut in the sill logs. These notches, whose positions should be first measured and carefully marked, may be made by ax or by saw, chisel, and mallet. The poles can stick out several inches on each side, or they may be cut flush with the outside of the wall if desired. Each juncture should be well spiked.

The objection to this system is that the sill log is weakened. One remedy is to spike or pin the joists directly on top of the sills, flattening the points of contact only enough to prevent rocking and to make a common level. The necessary notches are then

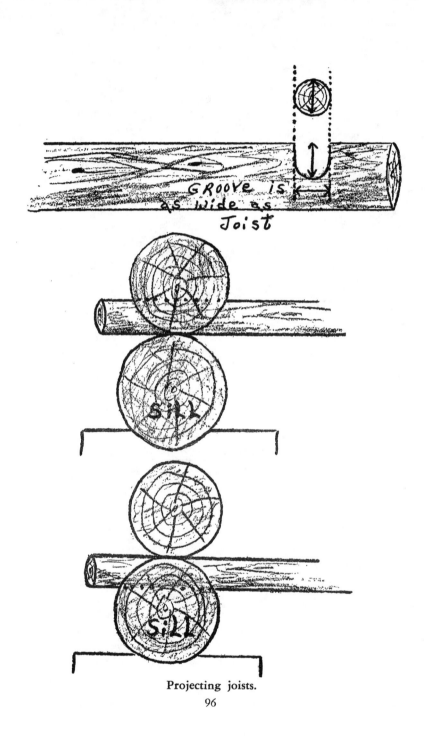

GROOVE IS
as wide as
Joist

SILL

SILL

Projecting joists.

96

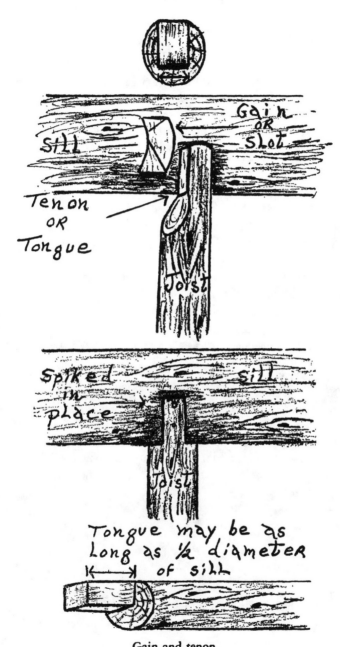

Gain
OR
SLot

SiLL

Tenon
OR
Tongue

Joist

Spiked
in
place

siLL

Joist

Tongue may be as
Long as ½ diameter
of siLL

Gain and tenon.

cut in the underneaths of the next two wall logs. Any discrepancies in fit are easily taken care of by caulking and chinking.

Some builders like to assure a more weatherproof building by going one step further, however, although a somewhat weaker floor structure is the result. The joists in these instances are not projected through the walls. They are cut instead so that they end about halfway across. The sill or the log directly above it, depending on which of the two methods are being used, is then notched only to the approximate middle of its diameter.

Gain And Tenon

A refinement of the above modification is the gain and tenon execution in which a tongue, sawed or hewed in the end of each joist, is inserted in a slot cut halfway into each sill log. The joists, their tops even with the tops of the sills, are spiked or pinned in place for additional security.

This procedure, although it has a workmanlike ring to it, has several disadvantages. It is unnecessarily difficult. It weakens the sills. It reduces the effective diameters of the joists and renders them liable to splitting.

Joist Specifications

Logs placed at two-foot intervals may be counted upon to provide solid footing if approximately six inches in diameter for twelve-foot spans, eight inches for sixteen-foot spans, and nine or ten inches for twenty-foot spans. Sturdy two-inch-wide milled stock spaced sixteen inches apart should be two inches deeper for the respective spans.

Few bushmen become so technical, which is why many a hinterland floor has a disconcerting vibration and an unnerving droop.

Sagging

A professional trick to discourage sagging is performed by arching the joists slightly. A lot of timbers, as a matter of fact, will be found to have a curve to them already. The more pronounced of these should be spotted at the center of the floor inasmuch as the most stress will be there. A center elevation of two inches will compensate for a twenty-foot span.

The more usual bush precaution, however, is to spot some rock supports about mid-floor and wherever else they may seem to be needed.

Trapdoor

Allowance for a trapdoor in the floor should be made now if, for instance, there is to be a small hole below frost level where such perishables as canned milk may be stored during cold winter nights.

Frontiersmen locate such caches as near heater and cabin center as convenient. Ventilation by means of a wooden shaft or a screened stove pipe leading to the open air is advisable. This will be stuffed closed during spells of extreme cold.

A frame to support the door may be made by spiking two-by-fours or flattened poles to and between the joists. The trapdoor itself will fit better if the floor is first laid to the further side of the desired opening, the door-to-be temporarily held together by two saw-guiding pieces of wood, and the hole then cut parallel and close to a joist on each side. The small rectangle should then be turned over and stout slats permanently nailed to it before the temporary holders are removed.

If there is to be a double floor, the hole can be opened and a similar cut made in the top floor when that portion has been reached. The frame can then be permanently spiked, the first thickness of the trapdoor set in place, and the upper thickness nailed to it. It is not necessary for both layers of the door to match exactly. There is more to be found on the subject of storage space in Chapter Sixteen.

Double Floor

Particularly important in the cabin intended for cold-weather occupancy is a snug floor. Vagrant drafts will otherwise be forever chilling feet and ankles even when the upper body is oppressively hot. Additional lumber put into a double floor will, in such instances, save many cords of firewood.

Finished Floor of choice, Laid at Right angles

Sub Floor of inexpensive Lumber

← Joists →

Water proof insulation Laid between Floors

Double floors are snug.

The sub floor may be made of narrow, square edged boards set about three-sixteenths of an inch apart to allow for expansion and contraction. If the wilderness home is very far from sources of supply, it will be probably made of whatever inexpensive lumber is available.

While it is technically true that sub floors are best laid diagonally so as to lessen the likelihood of any weaknesses or irregularities detracting from the finished surface, the added labor and waste of lumber does not always make this practical or advisable in log cabin work. It is generally better to install the double floors of the usual wilderness home at right angles to one another.

Waterproof insulation should separate the two layers. Heavy asphalt-impregnated roofing paper performs an extra function here by also discouraging the smaller woodland folk.

Flooring

The puncheon floor of pioneer days, made of thick hewn stock, is without equal in the log cabin if skillfully fitted and faced. That, unfortunately, is an increasingly rare condition. Pit sawn planks, actually or apparently fastened with wooden pegs, rank next in the opinion of many.

Lumber is the most practical product in most cases, however. It may be wisely used for flooring even if it appears in no other part of the rustic home.

Boards not more than six inches across are preferable to wider varieties. Random widths are in the colonial tradition. Tongued and grooved stock is used very, very successfully in many a cabin. So in a lesser degree is ship-lap.

Pine was the most common flooring in pioneer days. Today

such softwoods as southern pine, Douglas fir, western hemlock, western larch, redwood, western red cedar, southern cypress and hardwoods such as oak, maple, beech, and birch are widely utilized. The man on the cottage-dappled lake will be governed by taste and pocketbook, the man located back of beyond by availability.

Hard And Soft

The difference between hardwoods and softwoods is botanical, having nothing to do with the actual firmness of the particular species. Yew, a softwood, is much harder than many a hardwood oak.

may be scribed with compass,

Then cut to fit walls exactly.

Leave some clearance, however, so that expanding wood won't buckle floor.

First and last floor boards may be scribed with compass, then cut to fit floors exactly.

Generally speaking, however, a softwood floor is more suitable for the wilderness home. It is easier to lay, for nails should be greased or waxed before driven into hardwood flooring. Some hardwoods, such as rock maple, have to be drilled. Softwoods are less expensive, and they do not require costly and painstaking sanding or scraping.

Nailing

If the flooring is unseasoned, it will be advisable not to nail it permanently until the second year when it may be better fitted. Seasoned flooring is not always obtainable, especially in frontier regions.

It is usually not possible to fit flooring exactly to log walls with-

Set grooved side
next to wall

6 to 8 penny
Flooring nails

Another way to lay Joists
(half-groove and half-saddle)

Sill

Nailing tongue and groove flooring. Also another way to lay joists, half groove and half saddle.

out a lot of hewing, but this need cause no concern. Moulding, sometimes an inch-square strip, is generally put down later to seal any spaces.

The main thing to see to when laying the finished floor is that the initial board is true and straight. Then there will be less likelihood that good boards will be twisted out of line in mistakened efforts to make them conform with warped stock.

Narrow tongued and grooved stock should be placed so that the groove of the first board is against the wall. This side should be securely fastened by driving the nails straight through the board. The other side may be toenailed by six-to-eight penny flooring nails driven at an angle of about fifty degrees into the inside upper corner of the tongue. Cut nails will do for hardwoods. The added tenacity of coated nails is advisable for softwoods.

The tongue will hold the grooved side of the next board in place, and the tongue of that will be similarly nailed. All nails will be hidden therefore, those at each side of the cabin by the moulding. Any joints should be staggered. Boards can be driven into position without damage by inserting a short piece against the board actually being placed and hammering on that, at the same time standing on the floor board so that one's weight will hold it in position.

Nailing square-edged and shiplap flooring.

The final two strips ordinarily should not be nailed until the last one had been fitted and if necessary rip sawed. Then they may be placed with a ridge in the middle and tightened into place by having this ridge pressed together carefully so as not to crack groove or tongue.

Narrow boards with squared edges or ship-lap joints may be toenailed on one side and fastened straight through the board at the other.

A middle nail is advisable for boards more than six inches wide.

Colonial Effect

A colonial effect may be achieved by using planks of random widths fastened by countersunk screws. These should be topped by wooden pegs, tapped gently into place after being carefully whittled and then immersed in glue. Planing and sandpapering will finish off any protruding portions.

CHAPTER EIGHT

THE OPEN AND SHUT CASE

"Boil up some of those high-bush cranberries with a mite of honey," goes an Alaska Highway receipt. "They make better applesauce than prunes."

Substitutes are many in the wilderness. None, though, will successfully supplant a rugged door. The paneled portals of civilization are all right in their environment. Their effete delicacy is not for the log cabin.

Cabin Doors

A practical door for the wilderness home may be simply and satisfactorily made of two layers of boards or planks. The exterior thickness is laid vertically so that moisture will not be trapped unnecessarily in the cracks. The inner thickness is put on horizontally. Insulation, preferably heavy asphalt-impregnated roll roofing, is sandwiched between.

Too common, for no good reason, is the cabin door built of one thickness of preferably matched boards. Two horizontal strips, the upper one a half-foot below the top of the door and the lower about a foot above the bottom, often support this. A third cleat is sometimes added with improved results halfway between these two.

These latter doors are too prone to sag and warp. A more functional back is the Z type whose effectiveness increases with its width. The three-batten back can be strengthened by adding two diagonals to give each half the Z effect.

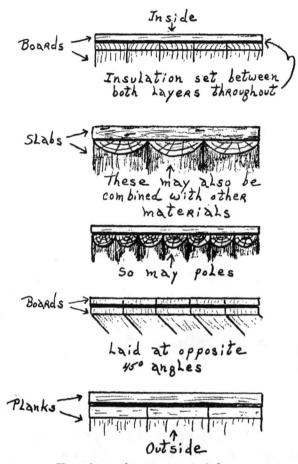

Inside

Boards

Insulation set between
both Layers throughout

Slabs

These may also be
combined with other
materials

So may poles

Boards

Laid at opposite
45° angles

Planks

Outside

Top views of some practical doors.

A one-layer door may be improved both in harmonious rustic appearance and in stability by surfacing its exterior with slabs or with poles. Small poles may be left round, but larger poles will fit better if flattened on one side. Commercial or natural insulation sandwiched in place will also improve this door. If thick waterproof felt is not at hand, for example, sphagnum moss should not be disregarded.

Wood

Handmade planks, whether hewed or pit-sawed, make the most appropriate door for the log cabin.

A milled plank can be made to look as if it has been sawed by two men standing respectively in pit and on platform. The trick is to have the mill roughen it against a buzz saw, after which it can be given a sufficiently functional smoothness with coarse sandpaper.

Going over milled planks lightly with a sharp ax, or preferably with a keen hatchet inasmuch as that can be more easily handled, will give them a desirable hewn appearance.

An impression of antiquity and long exposure can be imparted to cedar, pine, cypress, and other hard-grained woods by combing out the less resistant parts of the surface by means of a stiff wire brush stroked with the grain.

This feeling of age can be heightened by first scorching the wood with a blowtorch. Tests will reveal how far and with how much variance this should be carried so that the most desirable blend of antique browns will be brought out by the brushing. Two light coats of a good floor wax, well rubbed in, will help to seal this surface protectively.

Fastenings

Exterior doors in particular, since they are constantly swelling and shrinking because of the fluctuations of humidity and temperature, should be put together with long stout screws.

Nails will do, fortunately, although some discretion should be used in their selection when the builder is in a position to do so. A nail is a nail to many frontier storekeepers, who generally don't stock much of a variety.

Cut nails are heavier and more tenacious than wire nails. Unlike the rounded and pointed wire breed, cut nails taper to a chisel-like edge nostalgic of calmer years when men had the time and inclination to make nails by hand. The wedge-like tip should be driven in across the grain of the wood to minimize any tendency toward splitting.

The cut nail which imparts to the modern cabin door the heartiest impression of buckskin and flintlock days is the clout nail. The broad distinguished head of this has a high center which at the last sharp blow of the hammer embeds it firmly in the door.

The main characteristic of a clinch nail, also valuable but not so comely for door building, is its soft steel shank. This reverts inward, drawing and clinching the wood firmly together, when the point touches a metal face awaiting it on the other side. Doors so nailed are often put together atop the broad blade of a crosscut saw laid on the cabin floor. Or the side of an ax can be used to turn the point.

Dimensions

The builder can make the doors whatever size he wants. He will probably be influenced by the individual wilderness home itself. Log cabins, themselves characterized by rakishly low and ruggedly broad lines, generally call for shorter wider doors than those befitting city houses.

This becomes additionally true when the builder decides to hold his two side walls to about six feet and, for reasons of symmetry and strength, does not want to cut more than shallowly at most into any of the four top wall logs. Then perhaps a doorway some three feet wide, with its top about six feet from the floor, is what he'll decide upon for one end of the cabin.

He's likely not to want to weaken the bottom log, either. The top of that one will be flattened somewhat and given a weatherproofing outward slant, thus transforming it into a doorsill somewhat more pronounced than the framehouse variety. One will get used to it, however, although feminine complaints may be heard for sometime to come because of sweepings gathered by necessity on a piece of cardboard instead of being brushed casually outdoors across a threshold of normal height.

The bottom log should not be deeply cut, actually. If a high sill is going to worry anyone unduly, the best solution is to install the joists so that the finished floor will be only slightly lower than the top of the base log where the door is to be hung.

No serious harm should result, on the other hand, if the top wall log is cut at either end of the cabin. The builder who has any serious doubts on the matter in his own case and who will be

Side View — Outward slant to drain water

How to make with saw, chisel, and mallet

1. saw → ← saw → wide enough to admit saw blade

2. Knock out with chisel

3. saw → → → → → → →

Rugged doorsill. How to make it with saw, chisel, and mallet.

happiest with a door approximating the tall eighty inches of the city dwelling can solve his problem easily enough by adding another round or two of logs to his walls. Wilderness homes offer so much latitude that everyone can be very, very happy.

The average log cabin builder will be able to save considerable time and self blame by making doors to fit the openings, rather than by constructing the wilderness retreat to fit the doors.

About Openings

The common procedure is to build the walls solidly and then saw out the openings. Initial cuts which will accomodate the saw are sometimes partially or entirely made in what will be the top of each opening as soon as that particular log has been fitted

Easiest is to build solid walls, then saw out openings.

and spiked into place. The rest of the wall is then laid up as usual. This is the easiest way of attacking the problem.

Some builders complete their walls, then bore holes with brace and bit at the two upper corners of where each opening is to be made. A keyhole saw is then inserted through each aperture in turn. The section of the top log is cut out. The remainder of the carefully measured opening is easily made in both instances with a crosscut saw, guided by perpendicular boards nailed along the inside and outside of the wall with the assistance of a plumb line.

Openings may be built from the bottom up. This practice is arduous and exacting, however. It generally proves additionally difficult to level the walls once the top of each opening had been reached. Wood can be saved in this manner, nevertheless. This economy will justify the other shortcomings in some instances.

The procedure is to set well braced window and door frames upon what will be the log directly below each. This log may be marked, preparatory to the cutting out of a flattened recess an inch or two deep to accommodate the frame. Each end of the recess may then be sawed to the proper depth. A slot wide enough to admit the saw blade for the horizontal cut may then be made

Framing in doors and windows as the cabin rises is tedious, but it saves wood.

by sawing another vertical slit near one of the other two and then knocking out the block.

Short logs can then be fitted and spiked against the frames. Each should be spiked at least twice to each side piece or jamb. A single spike becomes a pivot on which the log can turn.

Frames

Regular lumber simplifies framing. Sound planks, about two inches thick, combine stability with appearance. These can be worked over with a hatchet, knife, ax, adz, or wide chisel to impart to them some of the well hewn splendor of pioneer days.

A sturdy doorsill is made by hewing the lower log itself. A slight outward slant will assure proper drainage. Such work need not be done by ax. A saw may be used in the manner explained three paragraphs before. Or one may employ chisel, plane, or other tools in ways detailed elsewhere and noted in the index.

Windows need a sill that will carry water out beyond the cabin wall, on the other hand, or the logs will be stained and the chinking weakened by storms. Lumber will take care of this easily enough.

Flattening the underside of the top log makes the stanchest lintel for both. Lumber is often nailed to the still round top log instead and chinked to exclude drafts.

If window, shutter, door, or screen door is to swing flat against any wall, now is the time to take that into consideration. The frame in such an instance must be set flush with the furthest bulge of the particular side of that wall. When one log curves far beyond its fellows, it may save time to reduce this extreme by a judicious bit of planing, shaving, sawing, chiseling, or hewing.

Stops

Stops are provided by nailing quartered poles or appropriate strips of wood around the inside of the frame so that the mobile section—window, door, or whatever it may be—will butt squarely against them when closed. This is best done by actual experimentation rather than by measuring. Set a door in place, that is. Then adjust the stops against it.

Trim

Because interior and exterior trim has long been installed in picture-frame fashion around windows and doors of city houses, that is no reason why the procedure need be aped in the well constructed log cabin.

Window and door trim unnecessary in well-built cabin.

If the junctures are very rough, although generally they should not be if care has been taken, it may be well to caulk and chink them tightly and then to guard further against possible drafts by nailing on trimming, behind which additional caulking has been pressed. This will necessitate the frame's being reasonably flush with the wall wherever such trim is added. This in turn may require some hewing, another good reason for avoiding the extra frill whenever possible.

Dutch door.

Dutch Doors

Dutch doors are often seen in backwoods cabins, particularly when there is a shortage of windows. These are most easily effected by sawing a full door in two after it has been already hung with four hinges, then taken down. Care should be taken to make and hang the Dutch door so that the top half will open independently of the lower portion. The construction will therefore vary slightly, as some cabin doors open outward to save room. This latter arrangement, of course, rules out screen doors.

A convenient shelf may be attached to the top of the lower half, its edge being raised sufficiently to check drafts that might

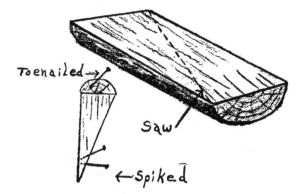

Rustic brackets for supporting shelves, etc.

come in through the otherwise open joint and also to prevent the top section from sweeping off dishes placed on the shelf to cool. Rustic brackets for supporting this shelf can be made by sawing a split chunk of log diagonally in two.

Hinges

Hinges may be made of wood. Two of the numerous methods are shown by the accompanying drawings. Anyone adopting either will be loudly reminded to grease the sockets well.

Leather straps, too, may be used. They will never rival the metallic tribe. A similar effect, particularly advantageous with heavy doors, may be achieved with iron strap hinges.

A search of antique shops will sometimes turn up hand wrought hardware cheap. If regular assortments are resorted to, and they are frankly far more satisfactory than wood or leather, it may be remembered that black ironwork blends in best with most cabins.

If the exterior door swings outward, it should be attached to the inside of the frame with butt hinges which fold over themselves when the door is closed and which therefore cannot be re-

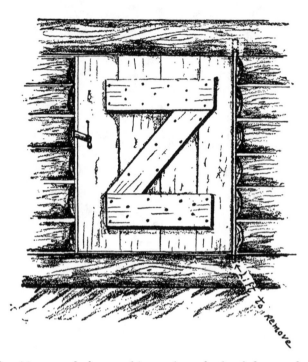

Wooden hinge made by attaching pole to back of door and riding
it in sockets bored in cabin logs.

moved in an effort to gain entry. These hinges can be fitted more
snugly if the position of each hinge is outlined first on the door
and afterward, when screwed there, on the frame—and a recess
equal to the depth of the respective wing of the hinge cut in each
instance with knife or chisel.

Cabin doors may well have a clearance on each side of the
frame equal to the width of a nickel. When the hinges are exposed,
the fitted door can be propped in place with the aid of these coins
as spacers and the other halves of the hinges attached to the cabin.

When the hinges are covered as in the case of butt hinges, the
fitted door is similarly propped in position and the upper and
lower dimensions of the hinges marked on the door frame. With
these as guides, a free hinge can be outlined in each proper posi-

Another example of wooden hinges.

tion. The partly open door can then be blocked or held so that one hinge, then all, can be screwed on in the correct location.

Latches

"My latch string is always out," had a neighborly meaning in olden days. The modern builder may substitute a thumb piece for the length of rawhide, but the wooden latch is as much an intrinsic part of today's cabin as log walls.

An affair of beauty as well as utility, the latch should be boldly treated as the illustration indicates. The pieces used in the making should be sufficiently well whittled as to merit conspicuousness. Attachment may be made by countersunk screws, their tops hidden by wooden pegs dipped in glue and then driven into place.

If a leather lace, which one's neighboring bushwhacker may refer to as babiche or shaganappie, is pushed through a hole and

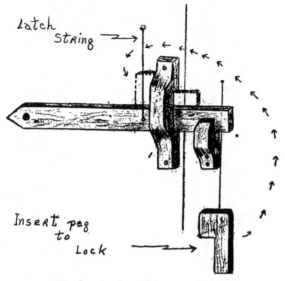

Wooden latch and how to lock it.

used to lift the latch, the door may be locked by merely drawing it inside. A wooden peg shoved between guard and bar will accomplish the same job and is an additional safety measure.

Metal latches are available commercially, and while they may seem to have certain artistic shortcomings when inevitably compared to those hand carved, they will actually fit in very well indeed, either temporarily or permanently. Doorknobs certainly should not be used.

Secret Lock

If the door is studded with nails, a secret lock of sorts may be made by attaching the latch string to the bent end of a nail and shoving the latter into the hole so that only its head is visible.

Combination Lock

A unique frontier-style combination lock can be made by running three long screws through holes bored in the door and clinching each off-center in a separate hardwood block. The principle is that when all three blocks are not turned at a certain angle, one or more will catch against the door jamb or in a groove provided therein.

Operation, which may be accomplished with a coin or a blunt old kitchen knife hung nearby, is simple. Make a tiny scratch at

Combination lock.

one end of the wide deep groove of each screw. Consider the exterior of the door as a map. The top will then be north, the right east, the left west, and the bottom south. Then the combination may be remembered, for example, as east north-east; the top screw pointing to the right, the middle screw upwards, and the bottom screw to the right.

Wooden Bolt

Like its pioneer cousin, the wooden bolt should be built with painstaking boldness. Although a substitute for the latch in numerous respects, the bolt performs certain functions of its own such as fastening a Dutch door together.

Bolts may slide into guards or into holes provided in the woodwork itself. The bolt can be locked by inserting a wooden pin behind it as shown in the drawing.

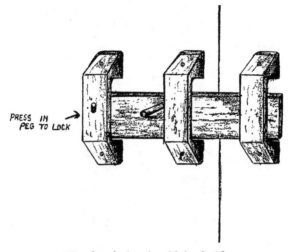

PRESS IN
PEG TO LOCK →

Wooden bolts should be bold.

Windows

Simplicities unsurpassed are the windows used in many a shifting logging camp. The centers of sill and lintel logs are slightly flattened. Jambs are spiked into place at each side of the opening to prevent the log walls from settling and breaking the glass.

Thin strips of wood are then nailed around the inside of the opening. A number of loose panes of glass are set against these stops. A second frame of stops is added behind these panes to provide grooves in which the glass may be slid to and fro.

Trapper Style

The trapper traditionally exercises moderation when it comes to windows. A grudging concession in overnight shacks may be a single small opening, screened and then covered with white cloth, greased paper, or a scraped animal hide. A tiny tear is sometimes reluctantly made in one corner of this in the interests of visibility.

Windows In General

The wilderness dweller should beware of having too few windows. It is often cheerful, comfortably warm, healthy, and exceedingly effective to have an expanse of glass along the entire south wall, plus additional windows perhaps at the southeast and southwest corners. One should think twice, particularly in northern climates, before allowing roofed porches to interfere with these.

There is no axiom to govern the actual selection of windows for a wilderness home other than that the sashes should be both

Casement window.

functional and harmonizing. Preferences, availabilities, and purses vary.

The casement window, which hinges into position like a door or shutter, is a popular choice that is particularly adaptable because of the fact that such a window may be made to swing inward or outward in any direction. If hinged on the side so as to open outward, it will combine the advantages of swinging out of the way and of being adjustable so as to deflect air currents into the house. The bottoms of sashes so installed may be planed to fit the angle of the sill.

Windows made to slide between tracks fashioned by nailing narrow strips of wood to the tops and bottoms of the openings are simple and effective. A usual method is to make the groove the exactly combined width of two sashes. Then two or more sashes can be moved tightly against one another and drafts and rattling largely avoided. Brief single-spaced strips at either end will hold the individual sashes snugly when closed.

Sliding window.

These varieties, plus the free window that is tilted slightly open or removed entirely when one wants ventilation, are the wilderness favorites. The extra space and framing required for proper installation of the conventional double-hung type militate against its log cabin use.

If the sashes available at the nearest wilderness community seem too small, the builder can always nail or preferably screw two or more together with the aid of cleats on both sides. This often has to be done in the woods, particularly to make the imposing stationary windows that are many times desirable.

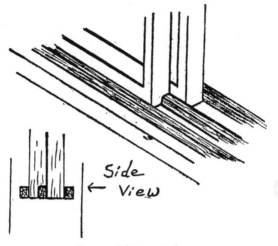

Snug sliding window.

Double Glazed Sashes

A vastly superior substitute for the old-fashioned storm window is the double-glazed sash. This incorporates two thicknesses of glass that are permanently sealed with an insulating layer of cleaned and dried air between.

Proof of their efficiency is the fact that the Hudson's Bay Company has successfully installed them in trading posts along the treeless Arctic shore where coal costs from $200 to $300 a ton and where wild free winds set snow whirling across the tundra like smoke, as if the North Pole itself were smoldering.

Screens

If the cabin is to be used only as a bivouac for ice-fishing parties, screens will not be needed. They will otherwise probably come under the list of necessities.

The simplest screen is made by tacking cheesecloth over a frame or opening. Cheesecloth's inherent fuzziness makes it superior to many costly screenings in keeping out that winged bite known as no-see-ums, midges, punkies, and well deserved profanities.

Thin strips of wood hold cheesecloth most securely. Thumb

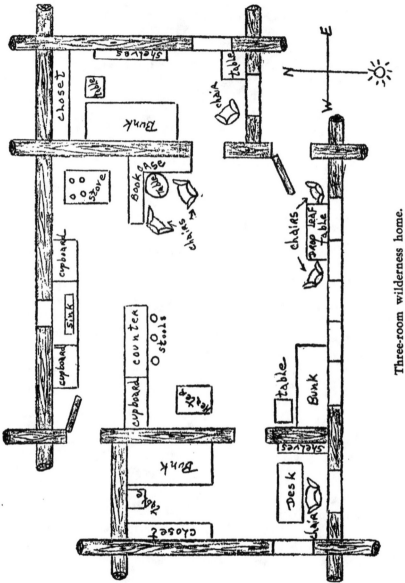

Three-room wilderness home.

tacks are good. If regular tacks are used, small bits of cardboard should first be slipped on to present a broad surface to the material. Tears may be repaired with adhesive tape. Cheesecloth is so inexpensive that the usual procedure is to rip it down when cold comes.

If the cabin has double sash windows, one may prefer to screen the lower halves only, affixing the cheesecloth directly to the bottom of the stationary upper sashes. This will permit unrestricted vision through the top glass.

Easily assembled screen frames are for sale. These are accompanied with readily followed instructions. If standard size openings are to be protected, all the paraphernalia necessary for making the finished screen may be purchased in one compact package.

Wire screen, to be effective for wilderness homes, must be finely meshed. The best obtainable screens have long been the bronze and copper fabrics which, in addition to weathering well and not requiring frequent painting, do not hamper the view as do the iron wires. The steady improvements in tough new plastic screens, which do not rust and which don't require painting, may well be investigated by the potential builder.

Screen Door

It is common knowledge that the screen door is made by covering with screen a frame reinforced with diagonal supports to prevent sagging. Not so many are aware that by temporarily shielding the same frame with canvas, the resourceful bushman transforms it into a utilitarian storm door when frosty weather arrives.

Philosophy

"It costs me nothing for curtains, for I have no gazers to shut out but the sun and the moon, and I am willing that they should look in," commented Thoreau. "The moon will not sour milk nor taint meat of mine, nor will the sun injure my furniture or fade my carpet. If he is sometimes too warm a friend, I find it better economy to retreat behind some curtain which nature has provided than to add a single item to the details of housekeeping. It is best to avoid the beginnings of evil."

CHAPTER NINE

TOPPING IT OFF

Roof that log enclosure and a cabin is created. Personal preferences once more hold the scepter. One of the sweetest joys in building a wilderness home lies not only in the satisfying of an instinct as old as life, but in the fact that a man can make it what he wants.

The Roof

One will do well to consider extending the wilderness roof four feet or so beyond the walls at each end of the cabin. This will not only enhance the low rambling appearance usually sought, but pleasant protection can thus be afforded door and stacked wood.

The eaves in turn, for balance as well as for storm-proofing, should be proportionately wider than those on the usual frame building. This motif should not be overdone, lest a darkened interior and a hound-eared aspect be the penalties. There is seldom the threat of this extreme, however. A far, far more common fault is the closely cropped roof which results in a pin-headed sort of deformity which lets moisture drip destructively over logs and chinking.

Solarization

Log cabins in particular, because they rarely do have such heating and air conditioning equipment as can be readily installed in city dwellings, should take the fullest possible advantage of the sun.

Roofs should protrude well beyond the walls of the wilderness home for this reason. When the sun is high in the sky during hot summer months, such a roof will shield the southern windows from hot direct rays without excluding light. These same eaves will admit the desirably warm low winter sun.

The desirable overhang of the roof varies according to the latitude, inasmuch as angles of sunlight change with the seasonal tilting of the earth at different degrees in different locations. How much of a visor the individual house should have may be determined by asking some observant native. Or an architect will usually be glad to answer this particular question for any specific locality without obligation.

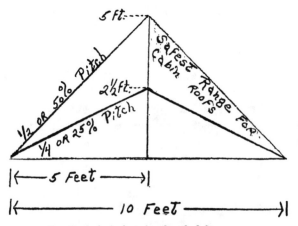

Roof pitch is height divided by span.

Pitch

Climate, construction, size, and design are the determinants in the matter of roof pitch. Materials, labor, and later fuel requirements increase in proportion with the steepness of the pitch.

The pitch of a roof is its slope or slant. The pitch, technically speaking, is the height of the roof divided by its span. These measurements are made from the plate logs, those top wall logs which directly support the roof.

When a one-half or fifty percent pitch is spoken of, what's meant is a slope that lifts one foot for every horizontal foot spanned. If the cabin is ten feet wide, for example, the ridge of the roof will then be five feet higher than the side walls. The height of such a roof, in other words, is one-half or fifty per cent of its width.

A one-quarter or twenty-five per cent pitch is a professional way of indicating that the roof slants upward from the walls six inches for every one foot spanned. With the same ten-foot-wide cabin, the ridge of this roof would be two-and-one-half feet higher than the side walls.

Log cabin roofs should generally range from a one-quarter to a one-half pitch. The former is usually sufficient for small well built cabins even where mountain snows lie long and deep. As roof areas and therefore potential pressures on it increase, however, so should the pitch.

One can roughly determine pitch in a practical fashion without bothering with try squares and mathematics. Measure the width of the cabin. Let's say again that it's ten feet. Therefore take from one-half to one-quarter of that distance, depending on the pitch desired. The roof, as already determined, will then be from five feet to two-and-one-half feet higher than the side walls.

Two things can now be done. Nail a board vertically at the center of one end wall. Measure the proper distance above the side walls on this board. Spike two boards at that point so that each will slant over a plate log. This will indicate the slant of the finished roof.

The same thing can be done on the ground to determine the angle of the roof. Mark on a log the width of the cabin. Nail to the center of the log an upright the height the roof will reach. Then angle two boards over the upright from the ends of the measured horizontal line.

Bushmen, in particular, often attack the problem from a different approach, angling boards up and inward from the tops of the side walls until what seems like a suitable pitch is indicated, then adopting that without any worry about percentages.

Plates

The plate logs are the top wall logs that directly support the roof structure. With an ordinary gable roof, the plate logs are the top sticks of the two longer sides. A pointed or a hip roof could be built, however, in which all four top wall logs would be plates.

The simplest and most effective top for the small cabin is the gable roof. This resembles an overturned V. The top logs of the two longer walls are then the plates. They are put up in the regular fashion except when corner posts are used. They're then spiked across the tops of these uprights. Plates for the gable roof are the same length as the ridgepole.

The Flat Roof

Flat roofs are more practical than one might think, although they are not to be recommended for heavy snow country. Sturdy construction and the relatively short spans called for by most cabins will avoid any danger from ordinary winter weather, however.

Waterproofing may be accomplished with roofing paper and tar bucket. A high-strength, heavily waterproofed felt is necessary. All joints must be tightly and thickly cemented. Additional protection can be given by brushing on one of the commercial bituminous coatings which are made for the purpose and which are guaranteed not to melt, crack, bulge, slip, nor support combustion.

One more precaution, not noticeable to the eye, is to slant the roof slightly for drainage purposes, say one inch for every ten feet.

One foolproof way to support a flat roof is by laying small logs across the shorter span at about two-foot intervals. Short logs, well caulked and chinked, will fill in the spaces above the plates. A picturesque effect can be achieved by extending the ends of these beams a foot or so beyond the roof itself.

A Sun Deck

A deck should be added to protect the flat roof if there is to be any foot wear. This may be made by nailing boards on flattened poles. Particularly effective and long lasting is canvas stretched over such a smooth, tight surface and kept well painted.

Unbleached, unsized, closely woven cotton duck is preferable. The weight may range from medium to heavy depending on the traffic. The duck is best lapped two inches and nailed every half inch with three-quarter inch copper tacks.

The canvas should be saturated with water and allowed to dry and shrink before it has been put down. Then the builder may work in a priming coat in which white lead in oil-heavy paste and raw linseed oil are the principal ingredients. Several coats of any suitable outdoor paint may then be applied.

An exterior ladder or stairway will provide the most easily made approach to the deck.

A Shed Roof

The roof with a single pitch is readily built. One procedure is to construct the front and sides of the cabin to the desired height, determine the slant by temporarily nailing guide boards from top to back, and then saw along the lines. Purlins are readily set in steps cut from the log ends as shown by the illustration.

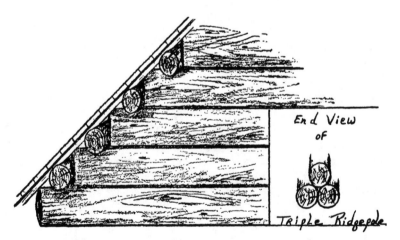

Purlins set in steps. Also end view of triple Ridgepole.

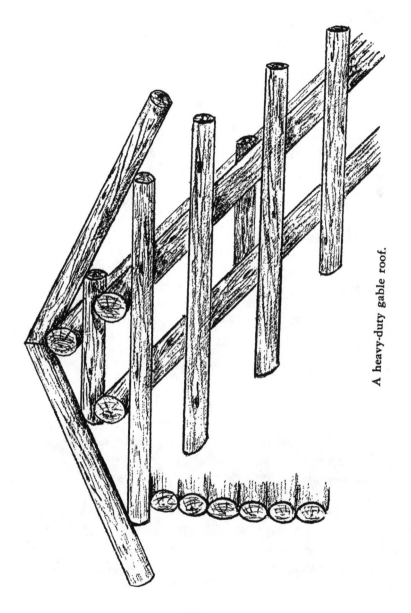

A heavy-duty gable roof.

Gable Roof

One bush way of building a gable roof is to run the ends of the cabin to the aspired height, center the ridgepole in notches, and then saw the gables into shape by following guide boards temporarily nailed from ridgepole to plate logs.

A more workmanlike procedure is to mark the pitch before proceding beyond the walls. Two boards may be run up and in from the plate logs and temporarily nailed in desired positions at each end of the cabin. Or two vertical poles extending at equal heights above the floor may be centered at each end of the cabin and guide poles angled from their tops across the side walls.

Gables are often covered with shakes, slabs, bark, or vertical poles. The ridgepole may be set on wall-supported vertical logs in such instances. Such vertical logs are also sometimes run up from rock foundations on the ground for stability.

A rugged and foolproof gable roof, especially efficacious when it is to be topped with heavy sod or dirt, is so simple to build in crisscross fashion that any attempt to describe it by words instead of by the following drawing would make it seem unnecessarily complex.

A Ventilator

A small, screened ventilator set in a gable will help keep the air in the cabin fresh, particularly when the wilderness home is left vacant for long periods. This ventilator should lie close under the protection of the roof so that storms will not beat in. A hinged cover, worked from below with a cord, should be provided to close the ventilator in frosty weather.

The Ridgepole

This crowning glory of the log cabin should be surpassed by no other stick in soundness, straightness, and sturdiness.

In snow country, use is occasionally made of triple ridgepoles —two poles laying side by side and reinforcing the top pole which is set above them in the groove thus provided.

Purlins

These horizontal roof supports, running parallel to the ridge, are usually no more than half the diameter of the ridgepole, but they should be sound and well proportioned.

If the gables are sawed or hewn into shape after being built, the simplest way to accommodate the purlins will be by cutting the ends of the gable logs in step form.

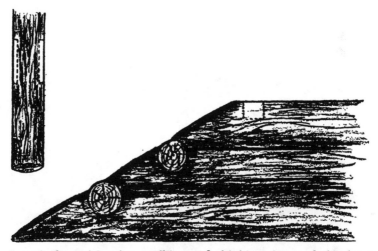

A method requiring less caulking and chinking. Saw and chisel out square notches to receive purlins squared where they pass through gables.

If the gables follow a predetermined pitch, the purlins may be set in notches as the work progresses. A maximum of neatness may be achieved by squaring those portions of the purlins that come in contact with the gables and fitting them in sawed rectangular notches.

Purlins should be bedded in moss or similar caulking for the sake of tightness. To conserve both labor and purlin strength, they should be placed so they will support rafters and other roofing without hewing or notching.

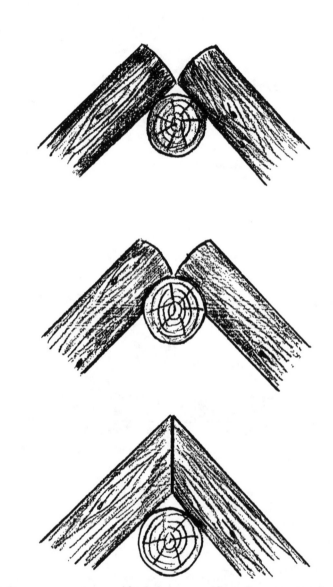

Rafters may rest on ridgepole, cup ridgepole, or meet in self-supporting angles above ridgepole.

Rafters

Running from ridge to eaves, rafters may either supplant or supplement purlins. When used without purlins, rafters are prudently placed about every fifteen inches. Poles used for rafters should average at least some six inches in diameter.

Ways of attaching rafters are numerous. The principle holds generally true, however, that the less the key roof sticks are cut, the stronger the roof will be. Rafters are discussed at length in Chapter Twelve, and the procedures outlined there may be adapted for log cabin use. Refer also to the construction and use of the mitre box as indicated by the index.

Purlins will sustain rafters without either being cut at points of contact if due allowance is made when the purlins are set. If either must be notched, it is preferable that the rafters be the ones tooled.

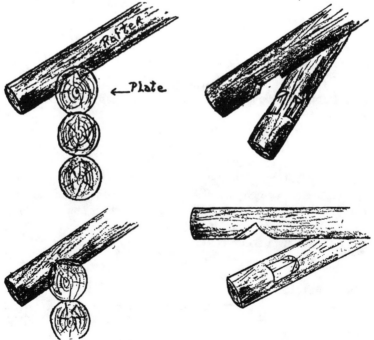

Rafters notched against plate logs.

Rafters may butt against one another above the ridgepole, may be cut to cup the ridgepole, or may meet in self-supporting angles above the ridgepole.

Notches may be made in the plate logs to receive the rafters which are then spiked solidly. Some builders use a lock notch for anchorage as illustrated, readying the rafters en masse on the ground after one pair of samples have been made true by trying and testing. Easiest of all is the butting of the rafters into eave logs without any notching of any kind.

The Eave Log

The eave log, although little known today in many parts of the continent, is a log of purlin proportions laid on the extended ends of the top logs of the front and rear walls. The careful builder flattens and spikes contact points or, preferably, bolts the eave logs into place.

The eave log is set at such a distance from each side wall that the ends of poles angled from ridge to plate butt securely against it.

The Pole Roof

Few roofs are more beautiful than those in which a layer of peeled poles, averaging some five inches in diameter, forms a visible part.

No cutting is required after the poles have been sawed to standard lengths if they are laid over ridgepole and plate logs so as to butt into eave logs. Some bushmen spike only the four end poles which may be larger than their fellows.

Such a roof, which is really a solid thickness of rafters, will scorn anything up to an avalanche, particularly if combined with purlins. It is not practical by itself, however, and is generally used as a base for further construction.

Beauty

A beautiful although fussy inner roof is made with short, small peeled poles laid over rafters or purlins that are about two feet apart. One section of poles slants at an angle of say 90° in one direction. The next panel slants at a similar angle the opposite way.

If care is taken to use straight and well matched poles, the effect is unusually striking.

Split Poles

A decorative although none too functional roof may be made by halving poles and laying them, rounded sides exposed, with waterproofing material sandwiched between. If the climate is mild, this may be but heavy building paper.

Trusses

These reinforcements serve little purpose in the small, well constructed log cabin except to provide a place from which to hang things.

Their usefulness as far as the builder of the wilderness home is concerned will be generally limited to roofs made of milled stock in high country. Steep pitch is not as much protection in mountainous climes as might be supposed. Snow has a way of piling so deeply around a cabin that heavy drifts are prevented from sliding off of any roof.

Trusses may consist of several poles running from wall to wall and each supporting one or more vertical braces. They may be as usefully complicated as a spider web. Rustic materials will improve appearances. The cabin may otherwise take on the aspect of a garret.

Gutters

Gutters in the bush are usually used only for trapping rain for washing purposes. Not being particularly decorative in most instances, these gutters are ordinarily confined to caches and other inconspicuous spots. Ways of making rustic gutters include the binding of birch and other bark to long rectangular frames made of poles. Split logs are also hollowed for this purpose.

Skylight

Many a good camping site is marked by a lobstick, a conspicuous tree from which a number of upper branches have been lopped. Many a cheery cabin is marked by a skylight.

The skylight frame may be built several inches above the roof

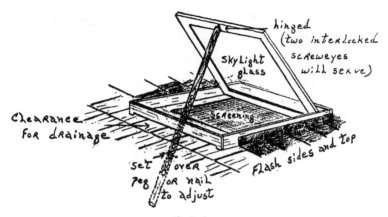

Skylight.

and flashed on all sides. A screen should be provided for use when necessary. Metal weather strips, attached to the top of this box frame and received by wide grooves chiseled in the sash, will further insure waterproofing. Clear safety glass made especially for skylights will permit unworried armchair contemplation of rain dripping spruces. A bored or notched pole, fitting over a nail, may be employed to keep the hinged skylight open at desired degrees.

CHAPTER TEN

INDIANS USED INSULATION

Ancient Ojibways, who habitually spent the cold months in tee-pees whose double walls were stuffed with moss, never dreamed that years later insulation would be considered a modern building development.

Roof Insulation

Insulating the cabin roof will do much to keep heat from beating into the wilderness home in summer and from escaping wastefully in winter. Earth, sawdust, and moss are among the insulating materials commonly available in the bush. There's also air.

An insulating sheath of inert air may be provided by sandwiching enclosed space in the roof. Poles and roofing paper, for example, may be separated by horizontal slats several inches thick placed between more roofing paper and shakes to accomplish this.

Double roofs, each complete in itself, proved valuable to American pioneers in the Southwest back in the early days of westward expansion. A regular plank roof may be laid and waterproofed with tar paper. Then, for instance, a few six-inch poles can be spiked across this as rafters for an entirely separate roof of boards and roofing paper, which will project over the basic roof like a parasol.

Moss Roof

Still common in some parts of the continent is the roof of heavy poles or hewn planks, topped with moss, mud, or sod. Such roofs

138

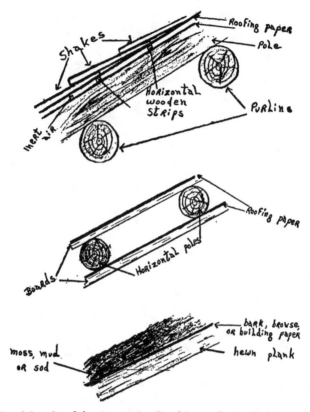

Roof insulated by inert air. Double roof. A pioneer roof.

are warm and inexpensive. They have an unfortunate tendency, however, to flavor slumgullion and other food if cooking pots are not kept covered. A layer of bark, browse, or preferably modern roll roofing should therefore be laid next to the wood to keep dirt from rattling down.

Careful builders, when forced to choose such a roof, sometimes protect it from the burdensome and deteriorating effects of water with a shield of shake-covered poles. When wind is more of a threat than rain, decorative flowers or a thrifty plot of grain are often planted atop the house.

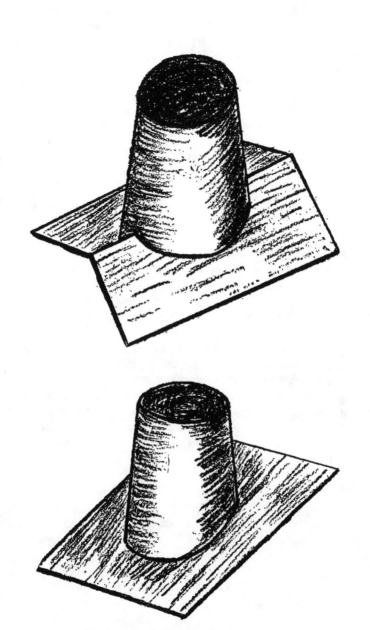

Two types of thimbles for stove pipes.

139

Smoke Outlet

The stove pipe should be considered before the roof is completed. Otherwise, as occurs a surprising number of times, it may prove easier in the end to angle it shiftlessly through a wall or window.

A safe way to conduct the smoke outlet through the roof is by the use of a double walled, ventilated metal thimble. If packed with some heat-resistant substance like asbestos, the thimble may safely be no more than four inches larger in diameter than the pipe. Otherwise the clearance should be twice this.

Light galvanized iron thimbles of single thickness are sold in most frontier general stores. One of these consists of a tapered tube, into which the interior portion of the stove pipe is fitted and over which the outdoor length is pressed, centered in a metal plate. The latter, nailed over a slightly smaller opening in the roof, serves both to flash the pipe and to keep it safely away from any combustible substances. It should be covered by the roofing material at top and sides and should itself cover the roofing at the bottom, so as to keep water from leaking into the cabin.

These thimbles are available with flanges so pitched that they will accommodate themselves to standard roof slants and still keep the stove pipe perpendicular. Rust and the swaying of the pipe in the wind, even when it is steadied by wire, make such lightweight thimbles short-lived. Inexpensive and easily installed, they should be replaced periodically.

Safety

It is very definitely advisable, particularly in the wilderness where hot wood fires quickly choke pipes with hotly and unexpectedly flaming creosote, to locate the outlet so that the pipe will rise perpendicularly from stove to open air. This is less important than having it arbitrarily pierce the roof near the ridge. It is usually an easy enough matter to add sections of pipe until the fire draws satisfactorily.

Chimney fires are always a threat in the woods, especially when greener and therefore proportionately hotter woods are used and when incomplete combustion results from fires that are banked so as to hold all night in cold weather. Pipes become clogged with combustible substances that can flare up any time. They do, and usually burn themselves out without trouble. The main danger is that this may happen when no one is present or awake to check anything that may go wrong. Clothing hung up to dry may catch afire, for example, and spread the blaze.

Some bushmen, particularly in the frigid regions where cherry-red stoves continually shove back the frost, meet this threat by deliberately burning out such creosote regularly. A fire hot enough to ignite an accumulation can be made by placing an old dry cell battery in the stove. Before doing this, of course, one should be prepared for any emergency. A chimney conflagration can be quenched, incidentally, by throwing salt atop the blaze in the stove.

All this emphasizes the importance of installing, whenever possible, heavily galvanized pipe with tightly locked seams, of conducting the outlet through the roof with the best double-walled ventilated thimble obtainable,—and of rigidly observing the other precautions recommended here and in Chapter Seventeen.

Flashing

Junctures in roof surfaces are flashed for reasons of weather proofing. The flashing may be improvised from any flexible waterproof substance from building paper and birch bark to flattened tin cans. The trouble with these, however, is that they are comparatively short-lived. So are some of the regular commercial flashings, such as galvanized iron. Flashing, although easily installed, is often difficult to replace. A sound axiom is to select a material that will last as long as the roof.

Aluminum, stainless steel, zinc, and sheet lead are all popular. Copper is good, too, and it has the additional advantages of blending in well with the rustic home and of being easy to work with. Flashing should be put on with rust resistant nails, made of the same metal as the flashing when that is possible.

Roof flashing is covered by any roofing above and at the sides. It covers any roofing that is below, so that theoretically water will never run under it. Chimney flashing is detailed in Chapter Twenty.

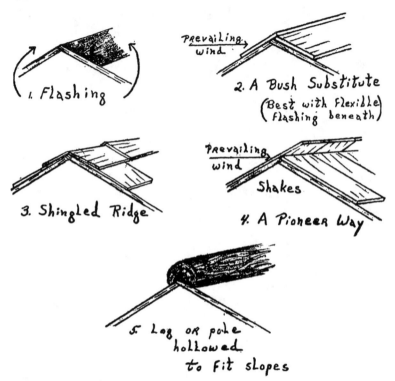

1. Flashing

Prevailing wind

2. A Bush Substitute
(Best with Flexible Flashing beneath)

3. Shingled Ridge

Prevailing wind

Shakes

4. A Pioneer Way

5. Log or pole hollowed to fit slopes

Good waterproofing insurance for any roof ridge. Five examples.

Shake and other pioneer types of roof may be picturesquely flashed at the ridge by a log hollowed in V shape to fit the slopes. An easier method is to nail two long boards together in a similar V. A common practice when the type of roofing warrants is to center a final strip of waterproof building paper along the ridge and fasten it down on both sides.

A Board Roof

The simplest practical roof is made of boards covered with as heavy and durable a waterproof building paper as seems consistent with one's budget.

If the camp is small, boards may perhaps be obtained in lengths that will run intact from ridge to eaves. They will otherwise go

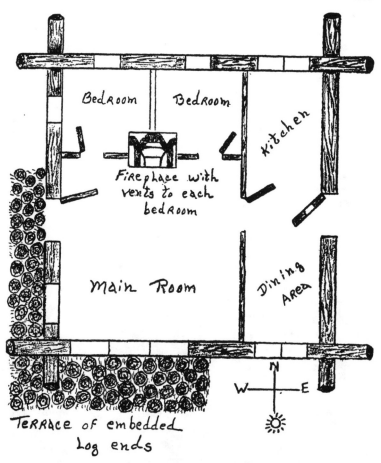

Four-room log house.

up most quickly horizontally, if the structure will permit it, the first length extending an inch or so beyond the rafters at one end and the succeeding lengths following suit. The other end may be left rough until the roof is up, then a guide board squared from ridge to eave in each instance and the extremities evened by sawing.

Interjoining boards, such as tongue-and-groove and in a lesser degree shiplap, make the tightest roof. No matter what sort of boards are used, some attention should be paid to turning them so that the best appearing side of each faces downward. Any roofing materials that are to be stained or similarly treated should be so readied while accessible on the ground.

Rust resistant nails are recommended for even the cheaper roofs. Heavily galvanized cut nails, two and one-half inches long, will do. At least two should be driven in at each contact point. Vertical joints should be well staggered.

Roll Roofing

The roll roofing is best laid parallel to the ridge. This work will start at the eaves and proceed upward, the final strip being centered across the ridge. Roll roofing, which is available in numerous grades and varieties, is the most quickly applied and the least expensive of all roofings. It is usually accompanied by nails, cement, and full directions for its most effective use. Details concerning such building paper and its application may be found in Chapter Twelve.

About two inches of building paper should overlap the eaves and ends of the roof so that it may be turned down beneath a finishing strip some two inches wide. This strip should be placed with a narrow edge flush with the roof's surface and nailed across the ends of the boards.

Shingles

Shingles and feminine hats vary greatly in style, composition, size, and cost. Wooden varieties traditionally are most in keeping with the wilderness scene. Cedar, southern cypress, and redwood are among the more stable commercial brands. The pines are generally good.

Certain drawbacks should be considered, however, before a wooden shingle is selected for the wilderness home. They are expensive, especially if the knotless edge-grain shingle cut from the heart of the wood is used. Flat grain shingles of varying quality are proportionately lower priced. They are also more prone to split, twist, and weather poorly. Then comes the labor and expense of replacing them.

Wooden shingles, too, should be treated with a creosote compound or some other preservative before being put up. The job of laying a shingle roof is fussy, too, when compared to some faster, longer lasting, and less costly roofing methods.

Shingling

The first row of shingles should be double and should project a half-inch beyond the edge of the roof. A little more than two-thirds of each row should be covered by the layer above. More exact specifications are for the standard sixteen-inch shingles to be laid five inches to the weather, eighteen-inch shingles with a five and one-half inch exposure, and twenty-four inch shingles with a seven and one-half inch exposure. The shingles will be placed, of course, so that the ones on top will cover the cracks between those below.

A professional trick is to soak seasoned shingles in water before placing them. Seasoned shingles that have been so treated, as well as those which are unseasoned, are spaced one-eighth of an inch apart to allow for expansion in wet weather. Dry seasoned shingles are separated by twice that distance. This will help prevent the shingles from buckling against one another when swollen with rain.

It is advisable to split shingles that are wider than nine inches, as otherwise they will be prone to split when in place.

Two inch-and-a-quarter rust resistant shingle nails, driven a half inch in from the edges and six inches from the top of each shingle, will suffice. Shingles in moist southern climates may be nailed on slats for purposes of ventilation.

Easy ways to lay shingles in a straight line are by butting them against a tightly stretched cord or a temporarily nailed guide board. Some prefer to snap a guide line into place with cord and chalk.

Shakes

Why not use the home-made oversized shingle, the shake? These can be split out of wooden blocks more easily than one might credit. Instead of attempting to rive them one by one, some builders halve the block, then bisect each half, etc. An ax is often used, but it need not be swung. The edge may be placed in position, and its butt pounded with a billet.

A froe, a heavy blade held at one end by a handle and hammered by a maul or mallet, will make the job easier. One can be inexpensively made in a few minutes by any blacksmith. It is set against a block that may be from two to four feet long, cut from a straight grained softwood tree that grew reasonably free from knots. Held a quarter-inch from the edge, it is driven in its full

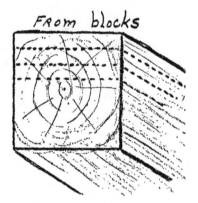

Shakes may be split from blocks and from split logs.

width, carefully twisted to start the split, shoved into the space thus gained and retwisted until the shake comes free.

Crude shakes may be cleaved from split logs and used with one edge left round. At the other extreme, conscientious craftsmen occasionally shape even better proportioned shakes with a draw shave, holding them perhaps in such an ingenious backwoods contrivance as the one pictured.

Backwoods contrivance for holding shakes to be drawshaved.

Shakes should be laid one or two inches apart. About a one-third lap is recommended for roof work, although bushmen generally seek to save work by stretching this.

Preservatives

Coal tar creosote may be used to preserve the wooden shingle or shake if a damp climate calls for such precautions. Avoid commercial creosote stains as, according to government tests, any value most of them have in checking decay is scant.

Shingles may be brushed, sprayed, or dipped in a solution of one part first-grade creosote and three parts kerosene. This should be done on the ground. Some builders, for the sake of appearances, prefer to dip only those portions that are to be overlapped. This will result in a cooler house insofar as the sun is concerned, as a light roof will reflect the sun's heat while a dark roof will absorb it to a greater extent.

Asbestos

Choice of expensive asbestos shingles for a log cabin for reasons of fireproofing is an unnecessary precaution unless the building is fireproofed throughout. These shingles, made of asbestos fibers combined with Portland cement, are extremely fire resistant and long lived.

They can be obtained with particularly appropriate surfaces, such as simulated cypress grain. These self-aligning shingles are usually accompanied by directions for installation and by such necessary accessories as rust proof nails and clips for anchoring lower corners. They should be applied over asphalt-impregnated paper.

Asbestos shingles are brittle. A hammer blow can shatter one. They cannot be walked upon, and therefore some type of support must be used by the workman laying them. Two lengths of wood can be nailed at right angles to the ends of a ladder, for example, and the ladder then hooked over the ridge. Asbestos shingles are heavy, so transportation expense combined to initial costs rule them out in many remote localities. Unless particular care is taken, they are apt to slap noisily in the wind.

Asphalt

Many have long ruled out asphalt and other composition shingles for log cabin use on the theory that such roofing is as out of place in tall timber as a gaudy beach umbrella would be on the wild shore of a glacial lake.

A few very acceptable brands of asphalt shingles are obtainable today, however, in the grain, color, and shape of cedar and other wooden varieties. These would seem to meet most such objections, particularly since these shingles rank next to roll roofing in simplicity of application, inexpensiveness, and functional durability.

Conventional square-edged shapes are most in keeping with the wilderness scene. These are obtainable in individual shingles joined by a common base. The proper laps are marked. Directions for nailing usually accompany the shingles, as there is some variance according to the size and weight of the particular material.

Bushmen generally lay them almost flush with the rim of the roof, letting them protrude about a quarter-inch at most. A more professional method is to support the edges with shingles laid along the outside of the roof and extending from one-half to three-quarters of an inch beyond it at ends and eaves.

Scoop roof made by alternating hollowed half logs.

Scoop Roof

Pioneer cabins were occasionally covered by a scoop roof made by alternating hollowed half-logs. The scoop roof is still more picturesque than practical.

CHAPTER ELEVEN

INNER SANCTUM

The walls of the log cabin are generally considered finished when caulked and chinked. They may be embellished to startling degrees, it is true. It is equally certain that red velvet sprinkled with brilliants may be wound around the center of gilded moose antlers, a treatment some taverns seem to favor. It's all a matter of taste.

Tedious wall work on a log cabin does mean additional labor. Furthermore, the effect in the well built wilderness home is too often similar to that achieved by wall-papering fine old paneling.

Weatherproofing

Log walls must be closed against wind and weather before the wilderness home will be habitable. This is so simply and easily accomplished that most builders take little heed of the spaces that remain between logs as the cabin rises except to limit them to a maximum of some two inches.

Log construction is sealed by caulking and chinking. Both terms are so intimately associated in cabin work that they are almost interchangeable. Caulking, however, generally refers more exactly to the setting of some elastic material such as moss or oakum in crevices. Chinking more definitely characterizes the subsequent blocking in of the filler by some rigid substance such as plaster.

Caulking by its elastic nature may be done at any time. Chinking should be delayed as long as possible unless already well sea-

150

soned logs have been used throughout. Sticks that have not dried out entirely continue to shrink diametrically when in place, widening cracks between one another. Plastering is therefore preferably put off until at least the second year.

Caulking

Oakum used for caulking performs a double duty, as its tar content discourages pests. Sphagnum moss gathered by the bag in nearby muskegs and swamps, other long-fibered mosses, cotton waste, burlap strips, rope, and similar materials are also used for stogging, as the bushman sometimes terms it.

Caulking should be strung along logs and bedded in notches as cabin rises.

Caulking is often strung lavishly between logs and bedded in joints as the cabin is built. Each stick is fitted first, then rolled aside a final time while caulking is spread along the log beneath.

This procedure is advantageous when abundant materials are at hand, if only because of the time it saves that otherwise would be spent driving in the filler later. Caulking so applied is tamped more firmly into position, and any excess trimmed off, upon completion of the building.

It is well to cradle, at the very least, all but the most tightly fitting notches with caulking as they are built. This will do away with some otherwise vagrant air currents. Caulking, too, should be generously concealed around door and window structures and in other inaccessible spots where drafts may develop.

All necessary caulking, in the case of well fitting saddled or grooved logs, will be completed as the tiers rise, as discussed elsewhere in some detail. Anyone bothering to groove fitted, seasoned logs may be willing to go to the additional trouble and expense of securing enough old frayed heavy rope fibers to fit these furrows exactly. Impregnated with white lead before being inserted this will make a well nigh troubleless seal for years to come.

Spud

A spud, a long piece of wood flattened on one end like a chisel, is traditionally used for driving the caulking into cracks. A spud may be whittled from a piece of seasoned hardwood in a few minutes.

One notable characteristic among frontiersmen has always been a fierce and often contrary determination to do things their own way, so it is natural that spud dimensions should vary. About a two-inch blade at the end of a twelve to eighteen inch handle is a convenient tool for ordinary work.

Long thin wooden wedges are also improvised. Here, too, a dry hardwood will stand up better.

Regular chisels, their edges first dulled by file or grindstone, are also herded into service. They do not grasp most caulking as well as a softer, yielding wooden surface.

A wooden, leather, or fiber mallet rather than a metal hammer is best employed with all.

Chinking Tools

An ordinary small trowel will do to smooth chinking into place. Some workmen consider this triangular blade improved if it is cut into a rough rectangle approximately one-inch wide.

Most bushmen transport the chinking material, often clay mud, in a bucket from which it is slapped into crevices with the left hand and then flattened out by a trowel held in the right hand. This method is fast, effective, and less tiring than holding a mortarboard.

Use of a mortarboard is both neater and cleaner. It is even advisable when such ingredients as glue and sawdust are used. The chinking is lifted to the crack, on the mortarboard, then troweled roughly into position in sections until the board is emptied. The workman then puts down the board, goes back and smooths out the plaster.

A mortarboard is made simply enough from a thin piece of wood or lightweight metal such as galvanized iron. Inasmuch as it must be held, it follows that excessive heaviness should be avoided. A mortarboard approximating a foot in length by about one-third that width will serve handily. A centered block of wood can be nailed, screwed, or bolted on for a handle.

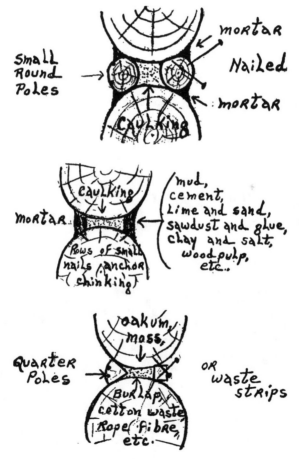

Chinking.

Chinking should be inserted, inside and out, in crannies that might otherwise admit wind and weather. This should be done in warm surroundings, as freezing and thereby expanding moisture will force this insulation out of cracks.

Chinking should be forced into crevices until it reaches the caulking material. It is important for reasons of warmth, however, that an insulative air space be left between the outer and inner chinking. A heavy core of caulking will, of course, assure this.

It will pay off in appearance and in function to trowel mortar chinking until enough water appears so that an apparently smooth, mirror-like surface is revealed.

Cleaning

Being too fastidious in the application of chinking does little but prolong the job. It is habitually more effective to go about the task with the boldness and heartiness which by force of environment has always trademarked wilderness construction. This infers no excuse for slovenliness. Most pioneer women, noted for their painstaking housekeeping, would never have stood for that and still won't.

Any chinking that drops or spatters is easily enough scraped neatly away and the log wiped immaculate with a damp rag.

Oil

The average log cabin, like the usual adobe home of the Southwest, has one peculiar shortcoming. That is its indisposition to stay clean. The judicious use of oil can often overcome this fault to a significant extent.

A thin coat of some inexpensive oil, as nearly colorless as possible so that it will not darken the interior unnecessarily, may be lightly brushed over clay, cement, and similar chinsings. It will tend to lessen crumbling and powdering.

Nails

Rows of small nails will help secure chinking. Hardening around them, it will thereby be anchored in place. Any inexpensive fasteners, such as shingle or lathing nails, will do. They may be driven in at about two-inch intervals. If a particularly stable chinking is used, such as cement mortar, this distance may be safely quadrupled.

The nails should be hammered deeply enough to assure their remaining solid even when bent up out of the way into a nearly vertical position. A half-inch insertion will usually suffice.

The nails should be set on the lower log along all horizontal cracks. Gravity will then also aid in keeping the chinking in place when logs settle, when they expand and contract during temperature changes, and when they shrink in diameter as seasoning progresses.

Metal

Strips of metal can be employed instead of nails to anchor chinking. Wire, too, can be tacked in crevices for the same purpose. Neither offer any marked advantage except occasionally that of faster installation. The fundamental object is to provide some sort of anchorage—if only the pioneer's rude, laboriously applied pegs.

Wood

Poles, whole or quartered, may be nailed in cracks. For even rougher work, some use the waste strips that many sawmills give to any who will haul them away.

These are all most satisfactorily employed to wedge crude, heavy caulking into wide cracks. Further weatherproofing is often done by then applying clay or other chinking. The chinking is compressed into a tighter seal, however, if applied first and, while still wet, backed by the wood.

Most such work is graceless at best and better adapted to log stables and caches than to well appearing living quarters. It is definitely functional, nevertheless, particularly if fissures are wide and if other available chinking will not weather satisfactorily because of inherent faults or because of excessive rainfall.

Rechinking

It becomes a pulse-quickening habit to check the chinking when almost overnight poplars become golden flame against incredibly blue skies, suddenly poignant with the din of swans chalking southward.

Old chinking that has started to loosen badly should be removed, carefully so as not to disturb any sound portions, and fresh material added. Actually, it is more often pressed back into place for another year behind a glorifying film of glistening new mortar.

Any tiny cracks, such as those often seen along the upper boundaries of chinking, may be gently closed with mortar applied with the flexible blade of a tableknife.

Mortar

Mortar used for chinking should be sufficiently stiff, no matter what its base, to hold its shape firmly against the tops of crevices until hard.

Mixing is most easily accomplished in a quickly assembled mortar box of the type already described in the chapter on cabin foundations. Only small batches should be readied at a time, so that none will solidify before being applied. Measurements need not be critical. Proportions may ordinarily be determined by the shovelful.

Tiny quantities for repair work or for testing may be stirred together in a dish or pail.

Some Are Cement

Cement mortar has been used long and successfully for insulating log cabins. More bushmen would avail themselves of it if it were not for transportation difficulties.

One part of Portland cement by volume may be mixed with two or three parts of clean sand. Fine sand will permit a smoother finish than will coarse. One part of Portland cement by volume, two of hydrated lime, and nine of sand will also make a satisfactory combination.

A handy stucco can be readied by merely stirring water prepared into prepared stucco cement compound which is available by the bag.

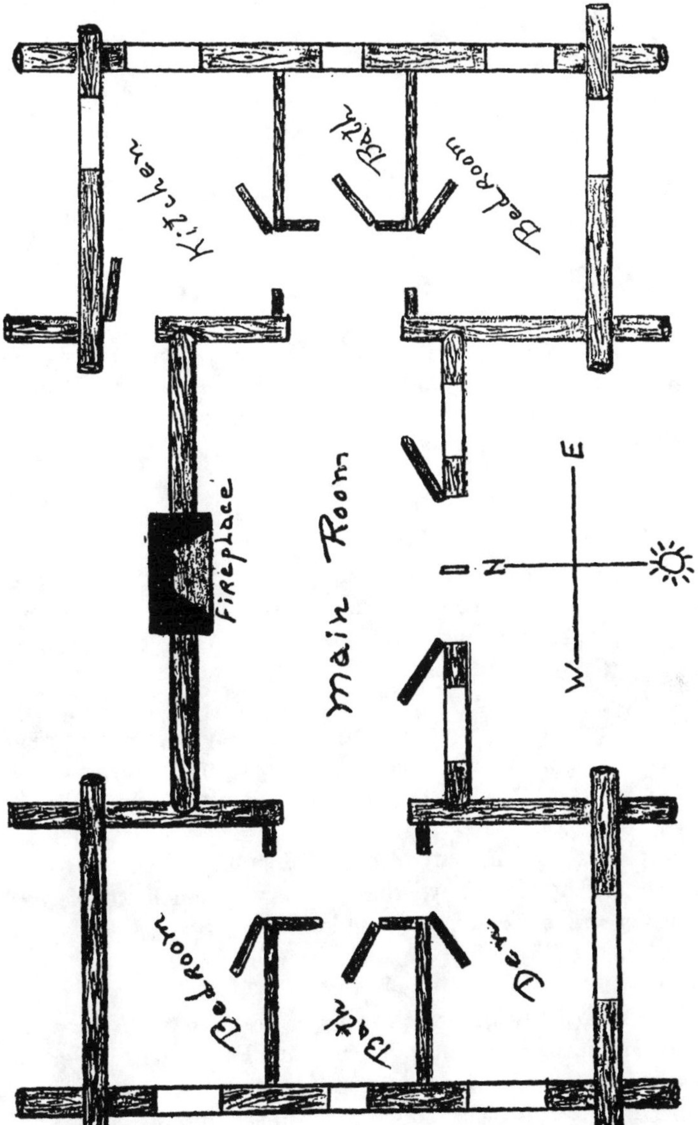
Kitchen
Bath
Bed Room
Fireplace
Main Room
N
W
E
Bedroom
Bath
Den

Five-room lodge.

Many Are Mud

Clay moistened to the consistency of thin putty was a pioneer standby that is still popular. Nearly every frontier community has its favorite local mud that is vociferously and militantly declared best for chinking.

At the first nip of Fall you'll see oldsters heaving shovels and picks in the backs of wagons for a clattering ride of several miles to a special pocket, perhaps distinguished from other clay by a cranberry redness or maybe a ripe yellow like marshgrass sweetened by the northern sun.

Clay mortar requires a great deal of hoeing, small splashes of water being added at a time until a thoroughly moistened firmness is achieved. If the mixture becomes too wet, additional clay should be added. Slushy mortar will settle away from the upper portions of crevices before it hardens.

Other Chinkings

Plasters of cheap flour, salt, and water are common in some sections. Sawdust is sometimes added. Clay and salt will do, particularly if augmented with a binder such as hair or sphagnum moss. Some trappers mingle short bits of grass with salt and wood ashes.

Few compounds are more harmonizing and functional than sawdust mixed with sheet glue. The glue is most easily melted, incidentally, in an old pan set in a basin of water which is then brought to a boil.

Newspapers may be shredded and then boiled into a tough pulpy mass. Anyone not wanting to go to so much trouble can mix water and packaged wood-pulp plaster.

Lime

Lime mortar consisting of one part of lime to every four parts of sand will make cheerful bright swathes. That is what Thoreau used when freezing weather threatened in 1845.

"I brought over some whiter sand from the opposite shore in a boat," he reminisced, "a conveyance which would have tempted me to go much further if necessary. I had made lime by burning

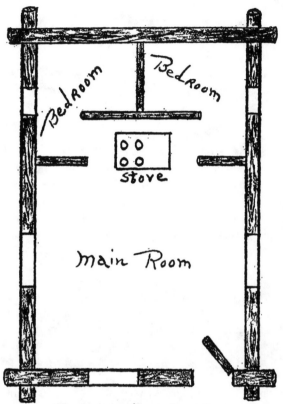

Heating a small sporting camp.

shells which our river affords. I might have got limestone and burned it myself if I had cared to do so.

"Winter set in in good earnest just as I finished plastering, and the wind began to howl around the house as if it had not had permission to do so till then."

Log Finishes

Most frontier cabins are still left as is. A notable exception is the Hudson's Bay Company's long practice of whitewashing its log structures. Approach a sleepy fur trading community, and the Company of Adventurer's trademark of snowy walls and red roofs is conspicuous as far as the eye can see.

Preservatives

Two or three coats of boiled linseed oil may be brushed throughout the finished cabin if the logs have not been previously treated. Not only does this protect the wood, but in damp climates it is advantageous in preventing the logs from darkening too drastically.

Drying may be hastened by diluting the first coat of oil with one-fourth of its volume in turpentine. You should make certain that you are buying boiled linseed oil. Inferior substitutes are marketed under purposely confusing names.

If the cabin owner is interested only in preserving the wood and does not mind darkening it, used crankcase oil may be brushed on yearly at little or no expense. Chapter Three contains a detailed discussion of preservatives.

Torch

Some like to bring out the grain of the logs by going over them sparingly with a blow torch. One should experiment with waste timber, however, before subjecting the cabin to this treatment.

Another use of the torch is in burning pitch in knots and coarse grains before varnishing or painting resinous logs.

Paint

Logs can be painted. Oak paneling can be papered, beams plastered, fine old fireplaces boarded, and little boys can decorate ancient sporting prints with mustaches. If one must have color, the best way to go about it is by adding a small amount of oil-ground pigment, purchased in paste form, to the initial coat of boiled linseed oil and turpentine. Natural wood colors are least objectionable. All sap must be removed from the surface of the peeled log before the stain can take effect, and this may mean laborious drawshaving.

Rooms

The most expert way to make rooms is to notch, or square, separating walls into place as the cabin is built. Squared tongues sawed on the ends of the inner logs can be quickly and neatly

Setting in log partitions.

set, for instance, in square slots sawed in upper and lower wall logs at points of contact. Walls may thus be erected solidly in, say, figure 8 form and all openings framed and sawed later. The easiest way to make rooms is by using partitions.

Heating arrangements should be considered if the cabin is to be occupied during chilly days. The solution in a small sporting camp may be the use of two sets of partitions arranged to conceal room openings so that circulation-blocking doors or portieres will not be necessary.

Partitions

Shakes, bark, slabs, and poles are among the rustic materials available for partitions. The plywoods, as well as some of the other specially handled commercial woods mentioned in Chapters Thirteen and Fourteen, are also very acceptable.

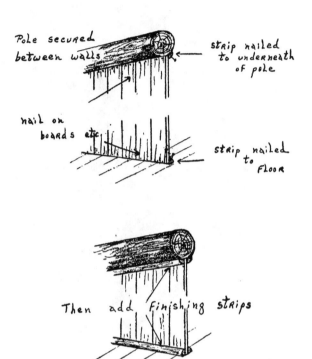

Pole secured between walls

strip nailed to underneath of pole

nail on boards etc

strip nailed to floor

Then add finishing strips

Board partition.

Shakes and bark may sheath one or both sides of light pole frames. For sound-proofing and insulating full length partitions, building paper may be put on before the exterior covering, and the space provided may be filled with sawdust or sphagnum moss.

Birch bark, particularly beautiful, is most easily applied after being soaked in warm water. Many will regretfully object to its extensive use, as it is very inflammable.

Slabs, when a single thickness is used, may be alternated so that the flat side of each will lap the flat sides of its two neighbors.

Peeled poles, set palisade style, will enchant many a sleep-lulled mind back to the days when voyageurs—using their bright sashes for everything from tump lines to swashbuckling tokens of distinction—sang beneath priceless fur bales.

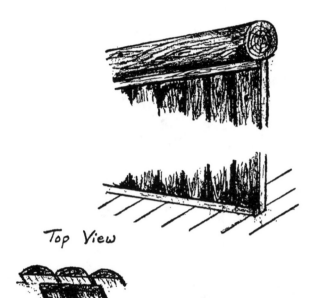

Top View

Slab partition.

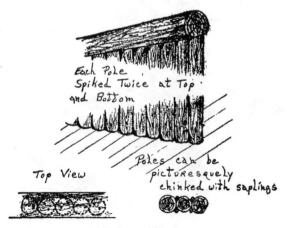

Each Pole
Spiked Twice at Top
and Bottom

Top View

Poles can be
picturesquely
chinked with saplings

Pole partition.

163

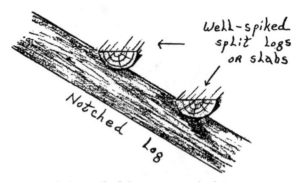

Stairs spiked between notched logs.

Stairs

An effective stairway may be made by spiking carefully smoothed slabs between slanted notched logs. Steps made of split logs can also be secured between two long split logs by stout wooden pins an inch or two in diameter or by large countersunk screws topped with wooden pegs. These steps may be further strengthened by sliding their squared ends into slots cut in the two side logs. Each of these gains is quickly made by sawing along two parallel lines, the width of the step apart, and knocking out the wood with chisel and mallet.

Rises in all cases should not be more than eight inches. Steps

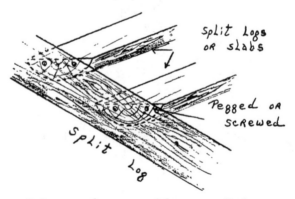

Stairs pegged or screwed between split logs.

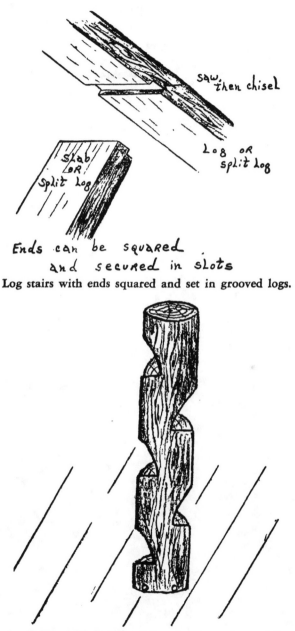

saw, then chisel

Log or split Log

Slab or Split Log

Ends can be squared and secured in slots

Log stairs with ends squared and set in grooved logs.

Pioneer ladder with hand and foot holds cut in upright log.

should be comfortably and conveniently wide. Or one may es-
chew these two particular considerations by adopting the labor-
saving ramp described in Chapter Twenty.

One simple pioneer version, particularly for access to a loft,
was foot and hand holes notched in the opposite sides of an upright log. Another was steps hewed or sawed in a single huge
slanted log.

CHAPTER TWELVE

CABINS WITHOUT LOGS

Fifty years ago less than four of every one hundred Americans lived in towns of 8000 or more. Now over half the population does.

Such quickly and inexpensively made shelters as those here suggested may afford some of these city-cooped millions at least week-end intimacy with God.

Slabs prove satisfactory substitutes for logs in many rustic camps and cottages. Shakes lend a genuine pioneer air. Bark, sod, adobe, thatch, clay, stone, tamped earth, and even railroad ties have their places. Telephone and electric light poles are excellent, particularly when stripped of old surfaces. Many a tar paper shack, too, is a vacationist's shelter supreme.

The pleasure afforded by even a lavish log dwelling can be multiplied by a well located bush retreat or two. A temporary or permanent lean-to, for example, may be thrown up in a surprisingly short time. The builder will often find one pleasant to camp in while working on his wilderness home.

Slab

Destined by innumerable mills for kindling wood or for discard, slabs may be obtained in numerous localities at give-away prices and often merely for the taking.

Slabs are in the same class as unpeeled logs. They may be preserved by one of the methods discussed in Chapter Three when threatened by insect damage. The inconspicuous use of large headed nails will help prevent loosening bark from later giving a ragged appearance. One for every square foot of surface will usually prove sufficient if one is interested in proceeding with this precaution. The slabs may also be peeled, and this will often seem desirable because of cleanliness when they are to be used inside the cabin.

Slabs, being merely the rounded portions sliced off the log when it is squared for sawing, have no uniformity. It is fortunately not difficult to square their edges by rip sawing, hewing, or planing. One generally has a large enough accumulation to select from, too, so as to be able to pick a likely looking batch for any particular building purpose.

Slabs with thick healthy bark are frequently used to give a rustic face to cabins built of scrap lumber. Such a structure should first be secured against drafts and dampness by as heavy and durable waterproof building paper as costs warrant.

When the frame of a shack is to be covered with slabs, a good idea is to pick a fair, still day and then tack horizontally upon one wall at a time as good a building paper as feasible, starting from the bottom. As soon as a wall is sheathed, vertical slabs should be nailed as tightly together as practicable over the paper with their flat sides down. The same thing is done with each of the other walls, rough spaces being left as framed for windows and doors. These may be trimmed later.

The builder can then go inside and sandwich the paper between a second thickness of slabs fitted against the first so that the flat sides of both meet. Particular care should be taken to space the second layer so that all vertical cracks will be covered. This sort of construction will progress a great deal faster proportionately on small structures where there can be a minimum of interfering framework.

Frame

Two-by-fours, since they can be used double when the occasion warrants, will do to frame the small wilderness camp not built of logs. It will be well, however, to use two-by-sixes or two-by-eights for the rafters. Poles will also do admirably. They are harder to work with, that's all.

The frame is merely the skeleton that, set on a sound foundation, holds the other building materials in place. Reasonable care should be taken to make it level and square. Only a very simple frame is required for a small, one-story building, as the illustration indicates.

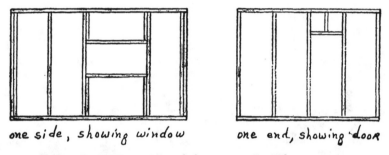

one side, showing window   one end, showing door

Only a simple frame is needed for a small wilderness camp.

The easiest way to go about the job is to sketch on paper just exactly what one is going to do before sawing a timber. Then neither motions nor materials will be wasted. One unskilled man can put up a twenty-by-ten fishing camp, with a double wall filled with sawdust for insulation, in a week if his materials are at hand. Two men can more than halve that time.

It is often handy in the woods to drop a couple of dead stand-

Cabin can be built atop skids, then dragged to new locations.

ing trees and roll them up on corner stones for use as sills. They may be left a few feet longer than the shack at each end. Heavy crosspieces can be notched and spiked between them at the extremities. Then a small narrow cabin can later be skidded away intact by truck or other power if such a move may be desirable.

A pair of well supported two-by-fours will serve for each sill of the small stationary structure. Other two-by-fours may be spiked on end across them as joists and a single or double floor put down, as detailed in Chapter Seven.

The floor will provide a base by which to measure and on which

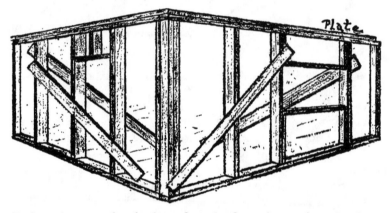

Each section can often be framed on the floor, then each set in place, braced, spiked to floor, plumbed, and finally spiked together.

to build the remainder of the frame. It will save time in most cases if all four walls are framed individually on the floor, then set up, temporarily braced, spiked to the floor, plumbed, and finally spiked together.

Each wall frame is primarily a rectangle made of four two-by-fours and reinforced by uprights some eighteen to twenty-four inches apart. Doors and windows may be framed within any rectangle by spiking in each case a pair of two-by-fours vertically the correct distance apart, then spiking other two-by-fours horizontally between them to make the top and bottom of the opening.

When the four walls are in position, it is a good idea to bind them more ruggedly together at the top by spiking an additional course of two-by-fours all around. Whereas the two end walls will set within the two long walls, these reinforcing end timbers will cover both butts of the two longer plates so as to make a firmer joint. Either a shed or a gable roof can be built, according to directions in Chapters Nine and Ten, with two-by-sixes or two-by-eights about two feet apart serving as rafters. If the gable roof is adopted, it will save time to fit these rafters to the bottom horizonals of the wall instead of to the less accessible plates inasmuch as dimensions will be the same. All rafters can be made on the floor to the accepted pattern. A board can be nailed between each pair to make an A which can then be handily spiked to the plates.

Rafters

Here is a precise and practical way to cut rafters, as shown in the accompanying drawing. It makes use of the fact that the shoes, the bottom horizontals of the frame, have the same dimensions as the plates which are the top horizontals on which the rafters will eventually rest. The method is so simple that the inexperienced builder in particular may find it expedient to ready the rafters as soon as the floor is completed, nailing the two-by-four shoes temporarily in position along an end and side for guides.

Measure the width of the cabin along the end shoe. Find the center of the cabin by dividing the width by two. With the aid of the try square, mark this along shoe and floor, so indicating the central position the ridge of the roof will later occupy above the cabin.

Now the builder will have to decide how much of a slant his roof is to have. This matter of slope or pitch is covered in detail in Chapter Nine. Briefly, the pitch is the height of the roof divided by its span. A twenty-five per cent pitch, for example, is when the slope lifts six inches for every foot spanned. If the cabin is ten feet wide, that is, the ridge will then be two and one-half feet higher than the top of the side walls.

The gable roof of a wilderness home should have between a

twenty-five and a fifty per cent pitch. If there may be a considerable snow burden, it will be more prudent to choose the latter.

With a fifty per cent pitch, of course, the roof slants upward one foot for every one foot spanned. If the cabin is ten feet wide, such a roof will be five feet higher than the cabin. The hypothetical ridge is already marked on the floor. Now measure five feet down one side of the cabin. Mark this distance at right an-

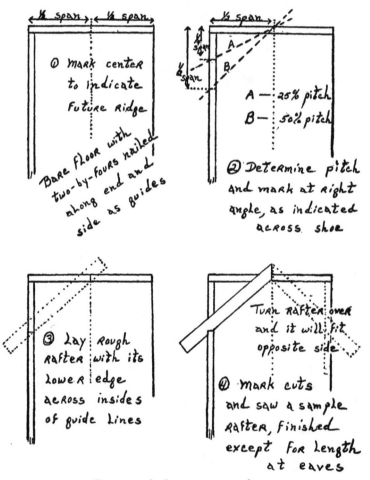

① mark center to indicate future Ridge

Bare floor with two-by-fours nailed along end and side as guides

A — 25% pitch
B — 50% pitch

② Determine pitch and mark at right angle, as indicated across shoe

③ Lay Rough Rafter with its lower edge across insides of guide lines

Turn Rafter over and it will fit opposite side

④ mark cuts and saw a sample Rafter, finished except for length at eaves

Fast, practical way to cut rafters.

gles across the shoes with the try square. That will indicate the rise.

Lay a two-by-six or whatever is to be used as a rafter across the end shoe and the measured side shoe. The lower edge of the rafter should pass across the inner extremities of the center line and the rise lines, as shown in the drawing. Nail the rafter temporarily to the shoes so that it will remain steady.

The exact slant that the rafter will assume when finally spiked in place to form the roof is now indicated. With the try square, transfer the center line exactly to the rafter. This will mark the place to cut this stick so that a second rafter similarly cut and reversed against it will form the ridge.

Take the try square again and transfer to the rafter the line on the side shoe that marks the rise. Measure in the width of the plate plus the width of the siding. If two-by-fours are used for the plate, the former will therefore be four inches. If boards one-inch thick are used for the siding, then one additional inch should be added to this. Drop a line back to the inner edge of the rafter at right angles from the end of the measured line. This will mark how the rafter should be sawed to fit squarely over the plate and siding.

An exception may be taken here if it is found that the seat cut indicated seems too deep. Allowance may be made only for the width of the plate. The rafters may then be spiked directly to the plate, and the siding fitted around them instead of being shoved under them.

Only one more consideration remains to be made. How wide are the eaves going to be? Inasmuch as the eaves are discussed at considerable length elsewhere as indicated by the index, let's decide for illustration that the roof is to extend an often satisfactory two feet beyond the walls. Lay the butt of the try square against the outside of the shoe. Move the try square until the two-foot mark touches the upper edge of the rafter. Mark that point. Indicate when the cut is to be made by dropping a line from it, parallel to the ridge cut, to the lower edge of the rafter. This bottom angle may be checked, incidentally, by laying against it the waste piece sawed from the top of the rafter when the ridge cut is actually made.

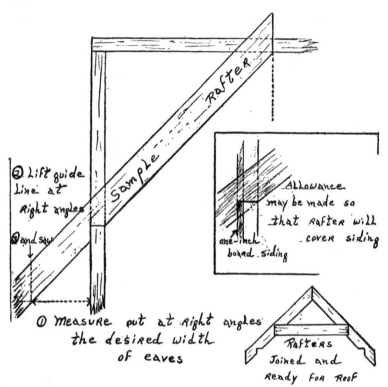

② Lift guide
Line at
Right angles

③ and saw

Sample

Rafter

Allowance
may be made so
that Rafter will
cover siding

one-inch
board siding

① measure put at Right angles
the desired width
of eaves

Rafters
Joined and
Ready for Roof

Width of eaves. Allowance may be made so that rafter will cover
siding. Rafters joined and ready for roof.

All that remains now is to saw out the rafter. Lay it back in
place, supporting the top with a two-inch wide block, and check
it against the lines on the shoes. If everything checks, use this
rafter as a pattern for two similar rafters. Spike these together at
the ridge. Nail a brace across them, making a large A. Make sure
they fit when set upright across the two side shoes. Then put
them aside until they can be finally tested for fit when the plates
are actually in place. If everything is all right, use the same first
sample for making all the necessary rafters.

If there is to be any painting or staining of rafters, do it on the ground. The same caution holds true for what will be the underneath surfaces of board roofing.

When the pairs of rafters have been set some two feet apart and held properly spaced by a board temporarily nailed across each side, the openings between their tops and the plates may be filled with boards or preferably more rugged two-by-fours whose tops should be planed or otherwise trimmed at the same angle as the rafters. This work should be done before any roofing is applied.

Tar Paper Shack

A tar paper shanty may be no architect's dream nor artist's joy. The inexpensive ease with which one can be put up will frequently recommend it, however. Never will I cease remembering with pleasure the nine-by-sixteen shack of this sort where eight of us, no less, paused a week while running the headwaters of the Southwest Miramichi River in New Brunswick shortly before freeze up.

Such a shack is usually made by covering a rude frame with rough or waste lumber, then shielding walls and roof against the weather with building paper that has been treated with tar or asphalt.

The paper should be applied horizontally from the bottom up, the first layer setting well over the sills to protect them from dripping water. No vertical joints should come much closer than one foot to any corner, as these spots are most vulnerable to moisture. The paper should lap a minimum of four inches horizontally, six inches vertically. It is smart to cement these joints with the adhesive that, together with simple directions, usually accompanies each roll.

Fastening this paper by broad wooden strips is preferable to the use of large-headed nails alone. The resulting difference in appearance customarily matters little. Wind and storm are too prone to tear paper away from the latter. When nails are used they should be spaced two or three inches apart along all edges. Whenever one encounters a hole, a good practice is to withdraw the nail carefully and to cement the puncture. Additional details have already been covered in Chapter Eleven.

The paper will bother less by wrinkling and bulging if spread out under the warm sun for several hours before application.

Building Paper

All frame structures should be sheathed with building paper whenever this is at all reasonable. The same methods of application as recommended for the tar paper shack should be used with the exception that large-headed nails, a container of which is often enclosed with each roll, will be used to tack the paper in place.

The market is replete with numerous grades of paper of various manufacture. These vary so considerably in utility and weight that the best guide for the uninformed buyer will probably be price.

When considerable time and money is put into a structure, there should be no compromise with the quality of the building paper. The building will depend on it to guard itself against drafts. The inner walls have to rely on it as protection from rain and moisture.

Rolls also vary in width, length, and area. Requirements may be quickly figured, however, from the specifications marked on each. Labels tell, too, if nails and lap cement are included. One-inch nails will do unless the paper, when used for roofing, is to be put on over old shingles. Then a one-and-three-quarter inch nail is recommended. These should have large heads that will grip the material without tearing. When exposed, they should preferably be rustproof.

Shakes

The tar paper shack may be given an artistically and functionally rustic appearance by sheathing it with shakes. The shake, which is an oversized wooden shingle usually from eighteen to thirty-six inches long, can be made by the wilderness dweller by any of the several methods explained in Chapter Ten.

Shakes used for covering walls should be laid about two inches apart, vertical cracks being covered by succeeding layers. The longer rust-resistant nails should be used, two to a shake. A one-third to one-half lap is generally excellent. Less is often used. This, however, sacrifices proportionately the marked insulating properties of shakes.

Bark

Bark may be cut into rectangular shapes for use in random sizes for sheathing. Some bushmen flatten and season it in sand for several months after peeling, as suggested earlier.

Paging Casey Jones

Some rivers are littered with seasoned hewn timbers, disguised as railroad ties. These may be set with one butt of each covered by the end of another, then spiked without tedious corner work.

Plywood

One must be sure to obtain exterior plywood if this modern sheathing, available in large labor-saving sheets, is to be used to cover the outside of a building. It is on the market in an increasing quantity of sizes and woods. Of the joints available, all of which should be bedded in a special lead compound obtainable at dealers, shiplap is perhaps the handiest.

Insulation

Wilderness homes built upon frames made of two-by-fours lend themselves particularly well to the use of insulation. This can cut cold-weather trips to the wood pile in half.

A dead air chamber, which will increase both summer and winter comfort, can be made by sheathing the exterior and interior of the house frame with siding laid over building paper.

Such a space may be transformed into a container for such inexpensive insulating materials as sawdust, obtainable at many mills for the taking. This can be poured into the four-inch-wide space from the inside of the cabin as that wall goes up. The eaves would interfere with insertion from the exterior.

A Permanent Lean-To

Few wilderness homes are complete without a guest shelter. A lean-to suitable for this purpose may itself be a forest haven, particularly acceptable to fishermen and hunters.

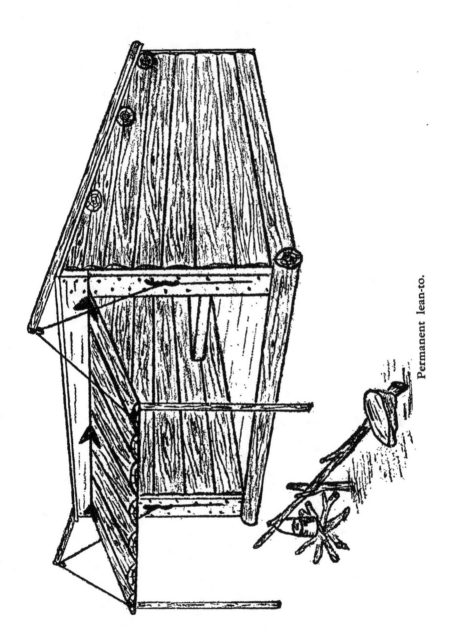

Permanent lean-to.

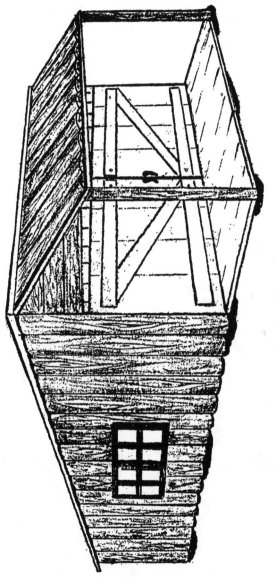

Another forest haven.

179

A functional design, with lines similar to those of the long popular Baker tent, is one incorporating a front that can be raised to provide additional shelter. When this lean-to is built of heavy rustic materials, particular care must be taken to make the hinged door light enough to be raised easily. A shed roof no higher in front than seven feet will conserve heat. It may be slanted to less than half that height in back where a long bunk will render additional head room unnecessary. A log across the front will deter floor drafts. A slab some eighteen inches from the ground will make a handy seat.

An outdoor fire cheerily reflected by back logs and upraised lean-to front will, after the evening meal is cooked, cast ruddy shapes invitingly on outspread sleeping gear.

Temporary Homes

Nothing is more enjoyable under favorable conditions than sleeping in blankets on star-silvered pine needles. There are other nights when a half-hour spent in putting up a bivouac is repaid in comfort, convenience, and refreshed well being.

One summer I spent several weeks in the northern Rockies with an anthropologist from the American Museum of Natural History, seeking evidence that the original Americans may have crossed from Asia to Alaska in pursuit of animals and then hunted the beasts southward.

We looked for once-inhabited shallow caves where, warmed by a reflecting fire in front, the aborigine might have lived in comparative comfort. Temporary shelters are governed today by the same principles that held true in the Stone Age.

Emergencies

"Where you are, with what you have, right now!" was Teddy Roosevelt's formula.

Perhaps a rock niche is nearby where a bough bed can be spread and a fire kindled. Maybe a few young firs can be angled against a fallen tree to provide a nocturnal citadel.

Evergreen Bivouacs

No difficulty in making camp by hands alone need be experienced in woodlands dotted with young evergreens. A knife or belt ax will make the task even pleasanter.

A stormy-day luncheon shelter is quickly fashioned by stripping the lower branches from a small evergreen so as to form a recess. The detached boughs, perhaps supplemented by others from nearby trees, can be used to floor and thatch the opening. Bubbling tea pail and sizzling kabobs will provide the final transformation.

The same motif may be followed in making an overnight camp. The tree should first be shaken free of any rain or snow in both instances. If one is traveling without blankets, thick layers of evergreen boughs above and beneath have a surprising insulating quality. So does birch bark which has the additional quality of being waterproof.

Lean-To

Even the more elaborate temporary shelters may be built entirely of bush materials. Rope and nails, however, will save time that otherwise would be spent in locating properly forked sticks and in providing additional bracing.

The wilderness home in hunting and fishing country is seldom complete without one or more outlying shelters. Boughs, bark, moss, mud, grass, and rocks all lend themselves readily to such structures. The only tool needed is a knife. A belt ax is even better. The heavier wood pile weapons automatically install their wielders in the master-craftsman class.

Snow

The fleecy white stuff can actually facilitate the making of temporary camps. Heaped around a rude lean-to, for example, it becomes a prime insulator and wind-break.

If one is among boulders, let him throw a bough roof over several that come closest to forming a natural cubbyhole. Bank snow at the sides. On a browse floor within, in the crackling warmth of a tiny rock-reflected fire, is snug sanctuary.

A rough triangle scooped out of deep snow, with the wider end roofed and floored with evergreen and with the opposite end confining a small fire, will afford warmth and relaxation even if one is without bedding.

Igloo

The snow house of the Eskimo often becomes the overnight shelter in "the only places as yet but little vexed by man." It is made of blocks sawed or cut from tightly packed snow. Additional snow is heaped and patted against the outside, as the blocks climb in spiral fashion. Snow platforms are built for sleeping bunks. A snow slab may form the door although, better, a short open tunnel curving downward and then upward will both confine heat and provide ingress and exit.

An experienced hand can put up such a snow house, large enough to accommodate a small family, in less than an hour if suitable snow is at hand.

The more permanent igloo may have snow wind breaks and a roofed anteroom to conserve heat and to provide storage space. Windows, generally facing south, may be sawed from clear ice.

Heat and light among the primitives of the twilight regions have long been provided by kudliks, shallow stone lamps burning seal oil by means of sphagnum moss wicks. The primus stove, colloquially called the puffer, is the modern version.

Tarpaulin

A tarpaulin, roughly nine feet square with four ropes on each side, is all the tent many want. Made of rugged waterproofed material whose weight can be held to about three pounds, it will serve as pack cloth, ground sheet, dining fly, and sleeping bag shell. It will quickly supplement a leaky roof or make two rooms where there was but one before. Readily does it become a sail for sled or water craft.

It may be pitched in the form of a low four-sided tent or a spacious canvas lean-to. By putting it up as a wedge tent and bushing the two open ends, it will cozily accommodate three abreast during storms and house a fortnight's duffle and provisions as well. Individual mosquito bars will afford comfortable nights during fly seasons.

Tents

The newspaperman's first-paragraph formula may well be considered point by point by the tent purchaser. "Who, what, when, where, why, and how?" There is no perfect all-around tent.

After deciding on the model, give attention to the fabric; whether it has been treated to resist mildew, if it is dangerously inflammable, how it must be handled in extreme temperatures, whether any substance has been added that will peel or crack, and exactly how waterproof it is.

Consider ventilators. Some tents become astonishingly stuffy during hot sultry days. A front that may be opened to a friendly fire and closed to a storm is not to be passed over lightly.

How is the workmanship? Have the corners been reinforced, the eyelets handworked, the ridge strengthened, the seams painstakingly stitched and—a minor but often indicative detail—are the ropes of good quality with the ends whipped to prevent raveling?

Encase the chosen article in a bag so that the container, not the tent itself, will bear the wear of storage and transportation.

Night Fire

That most genial of companions, the overnight fire, is customarily built against a reflector that may range from a convenient ledge to a wall of logs. The latter may be laid one atop the other against two slanting green stakes so that whenever the lowest log is consumed, the one above it will settle into place.

A long fire is preferable as it leaves fewer cold spots on the sleeper reclining lengthwise beside it. If one is short on bedding, the ground may be warmed before one turns in by kindling a temporary fire on it.

Slowly burning hardwoods make the preferable overnight fire. The resinous spitfires not only quickly flare to ashes, but their sparks are a menace. A veteran woodsman keeps a heap of fuel at his elbow. Half-roused by increasing cold, he stirs sufficiently to cast on several sticks, then resumes snoring with scarcely an interruption.

Old Logging Camps

Many an inexpensive and excellent hunting lodge stands unrecognized in the guise of an abandoned logging camp. Surrounding tote roads form a web of trails, frequented by the animals themselves, that may be softly and easily followed by the sportsman. Frequently one leads to a thoroughfare of sorts where a team may be hired to haul duffle and provisions.

Some building, generally the office, may often be converted into comfortable living quarters with the help of a few nails, some wire, a bit of white cloth or greased paper to cover a broken pane, and perhaps a roll or two of building paper to waterproof the roof for seasons to come.

Serenity

"Most men are needlessly poor all their lives because they think they must have such a house as their neighbors have. Consider," entreated Thoreau, "how slight a shelter is absolutely necessary."

CHAPTER THIRTEEN

SHUTTERS AND SHUTTERING

Shutters saved many a scalp during pioneer years on the North American continent. Today they guard numerous vacant cabins from paleface vandals and marauders.

Shutters also buffet cold and wind. On the well chinked cabin without double windows, they often mean a heat saving of up to twenty-five per cent.

Materials

Planks fashioned by hand—by pit sawing or by hewing—lend themselves to shutters that blend extremely well with the wilderness scene. Milled planks can be made to resemble pit-sawn stock by being roughened against a buzz saw. Touching them up with a sharp hatchet, on the other hand, will impart a hewn appearance.

An aged and long exposed aspect can be effected with surprising ease by the use of a wire brush on pine, cedar, redwood, cypress, and other well grained woods. The three-dimensional antique finish is imparted by raking out the softer portions of the surface by drawing the wire bristles up and down the grain.

Results are even more notable when the wood is first scorched with a blowtorch. Experiments will show how this can be variegated so that an apparently weathered blend of rich earthy brown will result.

One may also be able to secure sound old lumber which, even though it may first have to be cleaned, will fit in admirably with certain types of wilderness construction. Milled stock with the artificial patina of age is also available.

Ordinary lumber will do, of course, particularly if the shutters are to be in place only to close the cabin. Rustic facings of slabs or of poles may be nailed on otherwise if one wishes.

Construction

The function of shutters is to protect the wilderness home. They should be made rugged and sturdy with this in mind, decorativeness remaining only a secondary consideration.

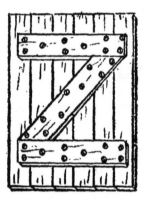

Four types of shutters.

The Z back is stronger than that made of two parallel cleats set horizontally at the top and bottom of each shutter. Whatever back is used should be applied so that it will not interfere when shutter is closed with it safely on the inside. Also eminently satisfactory is the shutter built of two thicknesses of board, one laid horizontally and the other vertically with waterproof building paper between.

Shutters may be built in pairs. This procedure is often neater and less unwieldy when the shutters are to be put up permanently. Using a single shutter for each window will, on the other hand, conserve labor and materials.

Screws or Nails

Shutters, inasmuch as they are exposed to the contracting and expanding effects of the weather, are most stoutly held together be screws. Not everyone will go to so much trouble, of course. Those of the latter sufficiently near supply centers so as to have some choice of hardware will do well to consider that some nails are superior to others for shutter building.

A modern version of the old wrought iron nail, and excellent for holding shutters tightly together, is the clinch nail. When this is hammered into place, an ax or similar metal surface is held so that when the soft steel point appears on the opposite side, it will be turned and clinched. Inasmuch as cabin shutters are generally put together on a flat surface such as the floor, the heavy wide blade of a crosscut saw can be easily enough laid beneath them for this purpose.

"Drive a nail home and clinch it so faithfully," Thoreau counciled, "that you can wake up in the night and think of your work with satisfaction."

Cut nails, which taper to a thin edge in a way reminiscent of the handmade nails common in a less hurried era, are stancher and more tenacious than ordinary wire nails. The wedge shaped end should be driven in at right angles to the grain so as not to split the wood.

The cut nail whose use perhaps best lends an illusion of early log cabin years is the clout nail, whose conspicious wide head is easily driven deeply because of a raised center.

Hinging

Shutters may be permanently attached to the cabin by means of butt hinges which will fold protectively over themselves when the shutter is closed.

The shutter can be made to fit more snugly if the position of each hinge is outlined—first on the shutter and, when screwed in place there, on the cabin—and an indentation equal to the depth of the respective hinge leaf carefully cut with knife or chisel.

The more tightly the shutter fits within the window space, the less opportunity vandals will have to pry it open!

Permanent shutters are most conveniently hung so that they can be swung back flat against the cabin. The frame in this instance must be set flush with the greatest bulge of the particular portion of the wall covered. When a log curves radically beyond its fellows, it may save time to reduce this extreme by hewing, planing, chiseling, sawing, or shaving.

A simple and appropriate way to prevent shutters from banging in the wind is by nailing or pegging a whittled strip of wood to the wall so that it can be pivoted across the shutter's front. This is a hewn variety of the old wrought iron S catch which, centered on an iron projection attached to the wall, is turned to govern the blind. Handmade copies of these may often be obtained at little expense since many frontiersmen still do their own blacksmithing.

When insulation against cold is not a factor, hinging shutters on permanently will result in many instances in an unwarranted masking of log work. Shutters and the window opening each covers can be marked with straight-line Roman numerals by chisel and mallet, and the shutters stored in a dry place until needed.

Closing

Shutters can be held closed on the inside by hooks and eyes. These, like other traditional hardware for the log cabin, should be heavy and substantial. It may be well, depending on the locale, to take pliers before shutting the home and to close each hook

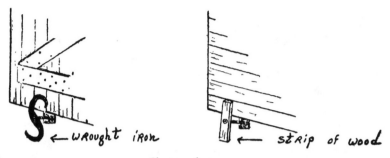

Shutter fasteners.

sufficiently so that it cannot be pushed loose by a stick or knife inserted from outside.

Bolts, particularly those that fit so tightly they have to be hammered shut, are not easily shoved open by intruders. Whatever fastener is used, one should secure the shutter at every free corner at least.

Extremes

Strong firm shutters, in extreme cases, can be locked over the window openings by bolts and nuts extending through the cabin walls. A metal bar should extend between each pair of bolts, across the face of each shutter, to deter prying.

Inasmuch as one extremity has been considered, it should be added that thousands of forest abodes are periodically left empty and unlocked for weeks, months, and years without anyone's presuming to do them the slightest hurt. This respect generally grows proportionately, it can be fairly added, the further the locality is separated from what some call our advancing civilization.

"I had no lock nor bolt but for the desk which held my papers," Thoreau said, "not even a nail to put over my latch or windows. I never fastened my door night or day, though I was to be absent several days. Yet my house was more respected than if it had been surrounded by a file of soldiers. The tired rambler could warm himself by my fire, the literary amuse himself with the few books, or the curious, by opening my closet, see what was left of my dinner and what prospect I had of a supper."

Fastening

It is well to fasten the windows themselves after shuttering the wilderness home. This may seem at first thought a needless precaution because its effect is more psychological than physical. The passerby who succeeds in levering a shutter will many times proceed no further if it becomes evident that to gain actual entrance he will have to break the glass. The shutter he can casually pound back into place without much damage, he may reason, but a pane that is shattered would remain as evidence of none too altruistic exploring.

Chimneys and stove pipes should be capped to exclude storms and pests, as suggested in detail near the end of Chapter Nineteen. Trapdoors and similar accesses will, it should go without saying, be secured.

Bush Code

The wilderness wayfarer, beset by emergency, may rightfully be forced to make a sanctuary of the cabin in the deep woods. Habitants, for this reason, often either leave such camps unlocked or provide adequately stocked shelter nearby.

Any unlocked outside doors should be wired shut, not tied, to insure their remaining closed until opened by human hands. Ropes are subject to the teeth of salt-hungry animals.

Locks

Even the better spring locks are nuisances on log cabins. Not only can they often be picked by sliding a strip of celluloid or birch bark between door and jamb, but they have a perverse habit of closing out unwary occupants. The similar but springless lock, which can be worked only by the actual turning of the key, is less hazardous.

Padlocks are the characteristic fasteners of the backwoods, partly because it is so easy to screw the necessary hasp securely in place. A well made padlock opened by a three-figure combination is handy, especially for locking doors for short periods of time. Also requiring no keys are the secret locks described in Chapter Eight.

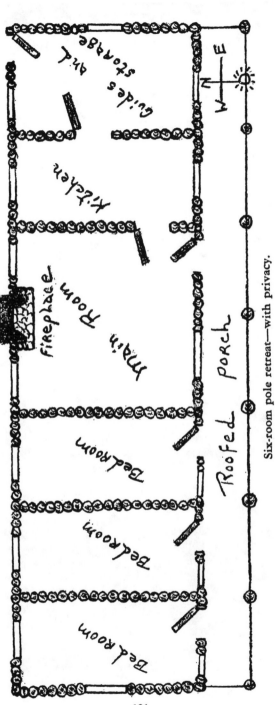

Six-room pole retreat—with privacy.

191

For a lock to go with barred and bolted shutters, bore a hole behind the door jamb. Make an opening in the door itself barely large enough to admit a hand and key. Then lock the door by means of a heavy chain secured by a stout padlock *inside* the cabin.

Good Old Days

Pioneers on some parts of the continent had an effective way of dealing with anyone who robbed a cabin. They escorted him to a river, tied him on a raft, and set him adrift.

CHAPTER FOURTEEN

FURNITURE IS FUN

"I would rather sit on a pumpkin and have it all to myself," said Thoreau, "than be crowded on a velvet cushion."

Furniture for the wilderness home should be born, not borne, there. Possibilities range from such simplicities as tables and stools to individualities like four poster beds. The particular cabin should be the arbiter.

Rainy afternoons can be enlivened by satisfying your inherent creative urge in the fashioning of seats and other necessaries for the forest abode. Furniture is fun.

Materials

Unpeeled birch is a favorite material for indoor furniture. Cedar is a top choice for all kinds of work, the rough sticks being particularly picturesque. Pine is certainly in tradition. The undisputed excellence of such hardwoods as oak and chestnut is tempered only by the increased difficulty you will have in working with them.

Seasoned wood is preferable, not only because it is lighter but because subsequent shrinking of undried pieces is apt to cause warping and wabbling. Many find it a profitable practice to store choice sticks to dry for future furniture demands.

Lumber

Planks can be given a hand-made look by having them roughened against a buzz saw at the mill, a treatment that particularly qualifies them for wilderness furniture making. Or they may be touched up with a hatchet, then rubbed with coarse sandpaper, for a hewn effect. Wood may also be effectively raked with a wire brush, perhaps in conjunction with light charring by a blow torch, as suggested in Chapter Thirteen. Lumber is not to be passed up too lightly, therefore, for such roles as table tops and chair seats where smooth surfaces are mandatory. Knotty pine is a log cabin favorite. Boxwood is handy for concealed work such as shelves and drawers. It is more desirable if faced with slabs or other rustic materials, however, when used for cupboards and such.

Plywood

Plywoods are available today in an amazing choice of varieties, some of which will enhance both the plainest and the most fastidious wilderness homes. There's natural finished vertical grain fir, knotty pine, and—among other beautifully blending types —handsomely rough combed redwood. Well made plywood has the advantage of coming in large, durable, lightweight, easily finished, exceedingly rugged panels which can be quickly and economically cut to any practical size or shape.

Cushions

The making of varicolored cushions will both brighten the wilderness home and make it more comfortable. Native fillers such as wild marsh hay, aromatic evergreen needles, and soft sphagnum moss may be stuffed in to make them invitingly plump.

One may even like to experiment with natural dyes. Cloth immersed in liquid in which swamp maple bark has been boiled will come out a mountain-lake blue. To make it a professional job, one needs only add a little iron sulphate to the solution first. If none is lying around the vicinity, a nickel's worth may be purchased from a drugstore. Or one may obtain some from a cobbler's shop where it is known as copperas.

Alder bark when boiled gives off a tawny yellow dye that has colored many an Indian's garments. The rich brown hue of pioneer homespuns was often obtained by boiling the outer nut shells and inner bark of the butternut tree. Sunflower blossoms contain a sunny stain the exciting hue of gold.

Glue

Waterproof glue in powder form is available for furniture building. When prepared according to instructions and applied thinly and evenly to tightly fitting smooth joints, it may be counted upon to make a union stronger than the wood itself. Other satisfactory glues may be purchased at almost any variety or hardware store. Directions accompany them. Glued joints generally should be kept under pressure for some four hours and not subjected to strain for an additional twenty hours.

Pegs

Nails will do. Screws are better. Countersinking the latter and topping them with glue-immersed pegs is finer still.

Elementals

A short upright log is the simplest stool. Place a slab, poles, or a hewn plank across two of these. There is a bench. Start with taller blocks, and a table is the result.

Refinements

Split a short log. Smooth the flat surface, using sandpaper to finish the job. Take a brace and bit, and augur, or even a jack-knife. Bore four holes in the underside.

Angle in four lengths of sapling or tree limb, about two inches in diameter. The tops of these should be whittled until they fit snugly. They can be fastened with glue, or small nails may be slanted through them into the slab.

An effective touch is to bore a small hole through the seat and each leg, then to secure the latter by driving in a wooden peg. Softwood dowels adapt themselves easily. Hardwood dowels have to be whittled with greater preciseness. Both will fit more solidly if first dipped in glue.

Stools so made often bring extraordinary prices at auctions under the guise of antiques.

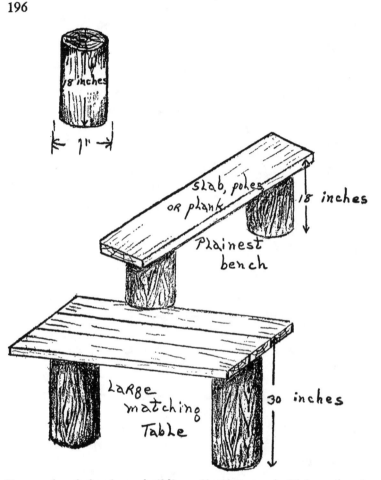

Elementals of furniture building. Simplest stool. Plainest bench. Large matching table.

Expansions

Handle a longer log similarly for a bench. Bore several holes in the flat surface to support a simple back, and a settee is the next step. Do the same thing with the stool to make a chair.

Longer legs will make a table. It may be necessary to brace the legs in these latter instances. Seat legs can be bored and rungs

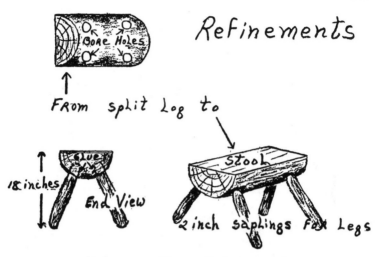

Refinements. From split log to stool.

inserted. A slab shelf can be screwed into position to steady table legs.

Other tops may be substituted for the original split log. Slabs will do. So will planks. Holes will have to be bored all the way through thinner woods, of course. This should be done from the top downward. When the tip of the tool pricks through, the boring should be completed from the other side so that the wood will not be unnecessarily torn and splintered. The legs after being fitted can be smoothed until entirely flush.

A spectacular table may be made from the naturally rounded end of a huge log that has been sawed some four inches thick. Effective companion tables may then be topped with similar slices from smaller logs.

Yardstick

Tables and chairs when used together may be respectively thirty and eighteen inches high. If the table is slightly lower, the differential between it and the chair will still be one foot. The backs of such chairs will be somewhat more than twice the seat height. They should be practically straight.

Attach Cushions
For Comfort

at least
12 inches

20 inches
or more

19 inches

17 inches

3 inches

Expansions. Bench with pole back.

If the seat and back are both pitched backward several inches, the seat lowered and widened, and a few rustic cushions added, the result will be a comfortable armchair in which to sprawl and lazily survey azure hills.

Motif

Simplicity is the enduring ideal to be stressed above everything else in wilderness furniture building. Actual designs may vary. When one is chosen, it is often pleasing to follow it throughout.

Effective is the use of substantial peeled poles of the same species as the cabin logs. Post tops need not necessarily be flat but can

Slab tops for tables and benches.

be slanted at forty-five degree angles and touched up with a sharp hatchet to give a hewn effect.

Well sandpapered slabs, left round on one side, will often fit in magnificently. Joints held by countersunk screws, boldly pegged, can many times add a final fine touch. Interlocking mortise and tenon joints, described in the following chapter are outstanding.

Checking

Some object to the cracks that open up in wilderness furniture. Checking may be combatted as suggested in Chapter Three. If one would fill the crevices, a mixture of glue and fine sawdust from the particular wood is good.

Uses of log ends.

Combination

"To eat is human, to digest divine." The simplest eating arrangement for the camp is a table with benches attached. Six poles and several slabs will do the job, as the illustration shows. An additional H support can be added to the middle if this seems desirable.

Similar combinations are enjoyably inviting when put up at outdoor vantage points. Four long posts are first driven solidly into the ground, and the piece is constructed around this nucleus.

Bookcase

A large or small bookcase for a log cabin can be built in a very few minutes if lumber is at hand. Decide first on the size. Assemble the four outer pieces. Then, perhaps using for a guide the books that are to be stored, mark on one of the side boards the

Window seat.

location of the shelves. Nail on small strips to support the shelves. Do this on the other side board. Fasten the frame together, nailing the sides inside the top and bottom boards for greater strength. Then set this frame in place against the wall, nailing it preferably. Saw the shelves to measure and slide them into place.

Simplest eating arrangement.

Blocks of shelves for any purpose may be rapidly assembled in this fashion. Add doors, and the result is a cabinet. Handy for keeping the doors neatly closed is a tiny magnetic catch which may be bought for less than a dollar or self improvised. A magnet, fastened inside the cabinet, attracts a metal plate attached to the door.

A more professional way of installing shelves is by sliding them into slots. These gains may be made easily enough by sawing in each instance along two lines, drawn the width of the shelf, and carefully knocking out the wood with chisel and mallet.

A—Saw top and bottom equal lengths.

B— Saw two equal ends to fit.

C—Lay ends side-by-side and mark tops of shelves with try square.

D—Nail on cleats. (ALL dimensions are optional.)

E — Nail outer
    frame together.

F — Saw shelves to
    one length and
        slide over cleats.

Building a simple bookcase in six steps.

1 - mark slot the width of shelf;

2 - saw,

3 - then knock out wood with chisel.

more Professional still

Professional shelves, and more professional still.

Drop Leaf

Drop leaf tables, both portable and stationary, are space savers. A frequently valuable provision, too, is a fixed cabinet whose door swings downward for use as a writing desk or typewriter stand.

Wood Box

The only trouble with a rustic wood box is in keeping it filled. Poles may be notched or nailed together in any of the several methods used for cabin walls. Wood boxes are sometimes made to slide through an opening in the wall so they can be filled outside.

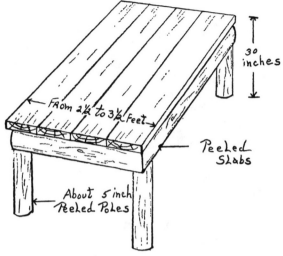

30 inches

From 2½ to 3½ feet

Peeled Slabs

About 5 inch Peeled Poles

A neat plank table.

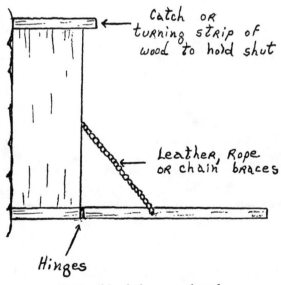

Catch or turning strip of wood to hold shut

Leather, Rope or chain braces

Hinges

Drop-table desk or cupboard.

Picture Frames

Quartered bits of birch salvaged from the kindling pile will do. Halved cedar saplings and the like are also excellent. Neat rustic frames may also be made of boxwood to which thin sheets of birch bark have been glued.

Covers of sporting magazines are often interesting enough to hang. So are some calendar illustrations. Maps of one's locality are invaluable. They may be secured from state and provincial sources and from the United States Geographical Survey in Washington and the Canadian Department of Lands and Resources in Ottawa.

Hides

Moose and similar hides not only impart a magnificence to log cabin furniture, but their smoky fragrance if Indian tanned will recall many a flickering camp fire. They may be used intact, or portions may be tacked to frames for chair seats and backs.

Rawhide Lacing

Hides may also be cut around and around with a sharp knife to form a continuous three-eighths inch or so lace for furniture making. An easy way to go about this is to stick a jack knife into a wide board. Drive a nail beside it the width away desired for the lacing. Then turn a piece of leather around and around this until it is reduced to a single long strip. This babiche or shaganappie, as it is called in the North Woods, should be soaked and stretched under pressure a number of times.

It should then be resoaked and, while it is wet, tightly laced to a frame to make webbed chair seats or backs. A snowshoe may be used for a pattern. A snowshoe needle, which can be interestingly made of a four-inch bone sharpened at both ends and with the hole in the middle, will quicken the process. Or the babiche may be simply laced back and forth over a frame or in parallel lines among holes cut in a frame.

The webbing, when dry, should be given several coats of high grade varnish, a process that may well be repeated yearly.

Restraint

Some care should be taken not to crowd the cabin too enthusiastically with furniture. Thoreau found three chairs sufficient in his wilderness home: "One for solitude, two for friendship, three for society."

CHAPTER FIFTEEN

LIFE IN BED

There are bunks built in niches and bunks in lofts, bunks that swing up against log walls in daytime and bunks that slide out of sight. There are wide two-story accommodations that demand most of the space in their particular cabins, lordly four-poster bedsteads, unassuming trundle cots, aromatic browse beds, and solitary hip holes scooped in bare ground.

Whatever his bed may be, man spends more than a third of his life in one. So it is a subject for more than fleeting consideration.

Decision

"It would surpass the powers of a well man nowadays to take up his bed and walk," said Thoreau, "and I should certainly advise a sick one to lay down his bed and run."

This condition need not be, although it is certainly true today just as it was a century ago in Thoreau's time. All the bed a man needs in the farther places—where he is more often judged for what he is than for what his furniture cost—is one he can carry beneath one arm, tie to an adventuresome pack, or roll behind a saddle. Such a bed can prove more comfortable and vastly more satisfying than the most sybaritic conventional contraption.

All will not agree of course even if they would trouble to experiment, since man's likes and dislikes are so often falsely and, therefore, all the more stubbornly bound by environment and by the convention of the moment. The same characteristic welds chains on the entire home-making problem, as it increasingly has since man selected his first smoky cave.

"People don't want scientific, comfortable houses," Ralph Linton, Yale anthropologist, noted at a Washington conference of the National Academy of Sciences. "They want to live up to the Jones, in homes that will knock their neighbors' eyes out. That's why there are Italian villas in Chicago and Cape Cod cottages on the Kansas prairies. To sell scientific houses, comfort will have to be made fashionable."

The owner of the wilderness home must decide for himself what sort of a bed he is to have. If he wants a manufactured spring similar to the one in his city bedroom, then he should purchase that first and build the bed around it. If he is to have what is, at the moment, a modern mattress, this should also be secured at the start so that the construction can be made to fit it.

Zenith

The largest sized eiderdown sleeping robes, light and incredibly warm, are as superior to most beddings as fine tapered fish line is to grocery twine.

Genuine eiderdowns are expensive. The lifetime of unexcelled service inherent in a good one will not always compensate the casual user. The individual who sleeps night after night in cold regions will, however, come to regard his eiderdown as little less indispensable than ax and matches.

As in the case of all essential equipment to be carried back of beyond, it does not pay the uninformed buyer to shop for so-called bargains. For one thing, all down is not eiderdown. One will usually want only the biggest and therefore most costly robe, as the small models are confining and uncomfortable.

If one uses an eiderdown robe much, the one trouble he will have will be the down's shifting toward the bottom. This leaves the upper portions of the robe vulnerable to cold. It often results in an inconvenient shipment to the factory.

The down actually can be redistributed immediately and easily. Open the robe. Lay it on a hard surface, such as the ground, with the lining upward. Then take a limber stick about three feet long. Beat the robe lightly from the foot toward the center. If necessary, turn the robe over and do the same thing on the other side.

Eiderdowns should be aired regularly, particularly in cold weather. When hung out, care should be taken to suspend them parallel to the clearly defined tubes. Warmth can be moderated in warm weather, it will be found, by lessening the frequency of the airings.

The Air Mattress

The well made, full size, air mattress is with a very few exceptions supreme in every department. Combined with a good eiderdown robe, it affords more sleeping comfort than one is apt to find otherwise on this battered globe.

The best, tufted air mattresses do not have any tendency to roll, incidentally. The several extra pounds one entails does rule one out for most back-packing jaunts, however. It is sometimes more agreeable in very chilly weather to spread a fur or other covering over one. This disadvantage of being cold on a frosty night is more than offset by unexcelled hot weather comfort.

Two common mistakes should be avoided by those fortunate enough to possess a pneumatic mattress. It should be spread preferably on a hard flat surface. If one wants to use it on an ordinary sagging bunk or even on a stiff but flexible spring, time should be taken to put boards beneath it. The best support the cabin owner can build for an air mattress is a solid wooden shelf about a foot longer and wider than the article in question. It's easy to comprehend how this will simplify the funiture problem. Poles will do, too, for the air mattress will hide minor irregularities such as those encountered when it is spread on the ground.

The second often repeated error made by those who occasionally use an air mattress is overinflation. The article needs only a little more air than is necessary to take the wrinkles out of it. The best way to prove this is to pump, preferably with a handy small rubber-bulb attachment that can be easily packed, until the mattress is well swollen. Then, lying on it upon one's side, the user can release air through the valve until one's hipbone barely touches the hard surface beneath. Then squirm around into different positions and see if that isn't the answer.

The Spring

No spring should be used with an air mattress, as has already been cautioned. If one is not going to use an air mattress, however, he may find it advisable to bring in a good new steel spring. The wilderness home should offer no sanctuary, certainly, to uncomfortable discards of any sort.

The steel spring may be supported in a box-like frame, across which several slats or poles have been laid for supports. The sides of the frame should be high enough to confine the spring and mattress and yet allow one to get in and out of bed without interference. The frame, which is best built especially to accommodate the particular spring, can itself be supported in a number of practical and often ingenious ways, some of which are later suggested.

There are purely rustic springs, of course. A rope spring, made of cord run back and forth across a frame, is the pride of many a locality. Such materials as canvas and burlap are often stretched into place. Small young saplings, sometimes fastened lengthwise but preferably crosswise between a stout wooden rectangle, make the traditional pole bunk of the bush. Springy boards and slabs are common.

The Mattress

The same thing that has been said about modern steel springs may be paraphrased for mattresses. Personal comfort and gratification should be the factors governing selections. If an air mattress is not going to be used, one should seriously consider bringing in the best and newest factory-manufactured mattress available.

There are rustic mattresses, too. Pine needles, well dried sphagnum moss, and sweet wild marsh hay are among the mattress materials native to the wilderness. Cloth containers simplify their use. The woods traveler often carries a tick which he fills anew at each camping spot.

Kapok

Kapok, which is a vegetable fibre used to fill such sleeping essentials as robes and comforters, will do for awhile in moderate climates. The material mats and powders with use, however, losing its effectiveness.

Fur Robes

Caribou and other fur covers play important roles in the night life of the snowy realms where they are made and used.

Lighter and more rugged than older versions of rabbit robes is the modern Indian's interpretation, made by shingling burlap with tanned whole hides lapped an inch or so. The pelts are then sandwiched protectively by a second layer of burlap. Anyone in the North during a rabbit year can make one.

Corner bunk with pole spring of wilderness.

The Bunk

The bunk, as differentiated from the usually movable bed, is built to the wall. The frame of the ordinary corner bunk requires no more than five poles at most. Since it has but one leg which supports the only corner not fastened to the cabin logs, it may be put up in several minutes.

If the entire back of a narrow shelter is to be converted into a single large bunk as is frequently done, the task is not much magnified. It is hunting and fishing shacks that are usually so equipped. The oversized bunk in one of these generally has a wooden bottom that is supported between a convenient log in the back wall and a single husky pole stretched across the front. This crosspiece is usually spiked between the side walls and prevented from sagging by one or two pole legs between it and the floor.

Height

The need for storage space is what usually governs the height of the bunk or bed constructed in the wilderness home. Such sleeping arrangements are often thirty or more inches high for this practical reason. The area beneath may accommodate drawers or shelves. It is many times found more convenient to store boxes, duffle bags, and even trunks loosely beneath.

The bottom of the frame can be closed in with boards or plywood in which doors or sliding panels are out. Easiest, though, is curtaining the space.

Two-Story

The double-deck sleeping accommodation saves space in a way more commendable in cold weather than in warm. Any cabin builder who has spent many nights in the top section of one will not make the mistake of adding frills which, although perhaps picturesque, will interfere with circulation.

The frame for the upper half of a double bunk may be made similar to that of the lower half, except that posts need not extend between corner and floor but can be spiked instead between corner and ceiling.

The upper story may be reached by a permanent or portable ladder which is also no recommendation. The former may be made of cross poles spiked between two vertical poles that are attached either to the bunks or to the cabin wall.

Trundle

The trundle bed conserves space and preserves sleepers from hot upper climes. It may be built atop four posts braced with crosspieces except along the inner length, so that the stationary bed or bunk under which the trundle is slid lengthwise can also

Two-story bunks with seat at side.

furnish a storage area. An end can be left open instead, of course, although more floor space will then have to be left unblocked.

Trundle beds for use in one room may be made to push end-wise through wall holes under permanent sleeping accommodations in another room.

Four Poster

A handsome four-post bed can be built entirely of seasoned wilderness materials in such a way that it can be taken apart in a few moments, then reassembled elsewhere in as short a time.

Dimensions will vary to accommodate whatever spring and mattress are used. A comfortable overall height including these, however, may be set at twenty-four inches.

Four matched posts, about five inches in diameter, will be needed. These will be worthy of a critical search. Four planks

Four post bed.

about two inches thick will be required, too. These may be roughed against a buzz saw or touched up with a sharp hatchet so as to have a handmade look. The posts should also be carefully worked over with a hatchet or ax for the same reason. The wood can then be smoothed down somewhat with coarse sandpaper.

For the craftsmanlike effect shown in the illustration, this bed should be fitted together with interlocking mortise and tenon joints held by removable hardwood wedges.

The bed spring can rest on slats supported by strips of wood preferably screwed near the lower interiors of the two lower sides. If the slats are made to fit tightly, their square ends will prevent their turning sufficiently to slip off the supports and will therefore make fastening unnecessary.

Mortise and Tenon

The mortise and tenon joint, besides being recommended for the preceding bed, can be very effectively used for tables, chairs, benches, and other furniture.

The joint is made with surprising ease, as the step by step illustrations show. The entire job can be done with a mallet and chisel. A small saw, such as a keyhole saw, and a brace and bit will make the work even simpler.

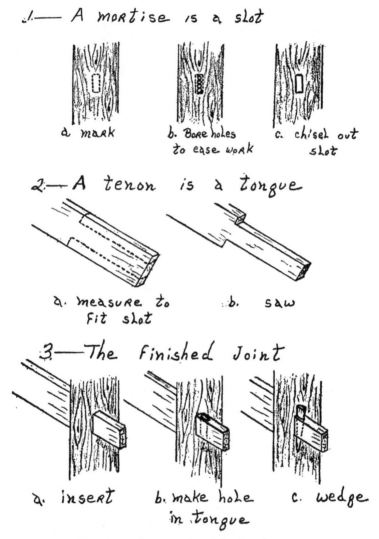

1.— A mortise is a slot

a. mark

b. Bore holes to ease work

c. chisel out slot

2.— A tenon is a tongue

a. measure to fit slot

b. saw

3.— The finished Joint

a. insert

b. make hole in tongue

c. wedge

Mortise and tenon, in eight simple steps.

The mortise is a slot which in this instance is cut in a piece of wood. A tenon is a tongue, made at the end of another piece of wood, which can be inserted at right angles through the slot. A hole is made in the projecting end of the tongue and a wooden wedge driven in to pin the joint tightly together.

In the use of the interlocking joint suggested for the four-post bed, each tenon may be marked on both sides of the wood with the aid of a try square, then sawed with a fine-tooth tool on the waste side of the guide lines. It may then be smoothed with sandpaper.

A slot just large enough to accommodate this tongue is then marked on one side of the piece of wood through which each is to be pushed. This location mark may be moved to the opposite side as well by the try square to assure accuracy.

The rectangular holes can be cut with a chisel and mallet, then trimmed with a knife and finally smoothed by sandpaper. The wood will knock out more neatly if a number of holes are first bored side by side within the indicated slot. These holes should not extend the full width of the mortise. They should be made by

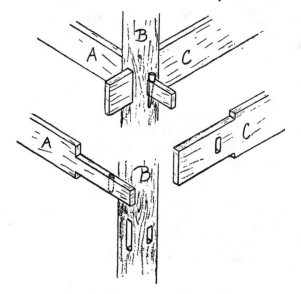

Interlocking tenon and mortise.

boring through one side until the tool pricks through, then turning the wood and boring from the other side, thereby avoiding splintering. A small narrow slot is similarly marked and cut in the locking tongue. A wooden wedge, whittled to fit tightly, is then driven in to hold the assembled joint together. The distance between the inside of this final slot and the base of the tongue should, of course, equal the width of the main mortise.

Browse Beds

Browse beds, common fodder to followers of romantic outdoor stories of the "ohh" and "ahh" school, are overrated. The bushman seldom builds one except for accompanying sportsmen, contenting himself more often with a hip hole when siwashing.

The real browse bed is not tossed down in a minute or two. It is thatched, a process requiring more like a half an hour. The springiest evergreen boughs obtainable are needed, preferably the smaller branches of the thick-needled balsam. They can be easily carried, incidentally, if laid one by one over the handle of an ax.

A deep layer at the head of the bed starts the ceremony. The boughs are placed with their undersides upward, opposite to the way they grow, and with the butts well covered and pointing toward the bed's base. Row after row is laid in this manner until the mattress is at least a foot thick. The bed is then made level and resilient by soft evergreen tips shoved in wherever possible.

The first night on such a bed is a sleep-lulling, aromatic ecstasy that everyone should experience at least once. The second night will be a bit bumpy. After the third night, one will feel inclined to attempt renovations with an ax load of fresh boughs.

Blankets

Hudson's Bay Company Point Blankets, made of virgin wool left rich in animal oil, are still unequaled for year upon year of use under the severest conditions. The present 3 1/2 and 4 points, (which at one time signified the number of beaver skins necessary to trade for them), indicate differences only in blanket areas. The material is of standard weight and quality.

It's whispered in the North Country that old trappers, who have deserted moccasin trails for village streets, can still hear the grizzly batting salmon ashore with sodden paws and the moose making his starchy meal of dripping lily roots when they pull a Point blanket closer around their ears on a snowy night.

CHAPTER SIXTEEN

HOT AND COLD STORAGE

The cache of the North Woods trapper or prospector is frequently a miniature log cabin, elevated on high poles which are sheathed well above snow level with flattened cans to bar climbing wild folk from ermine to bears. A platform which serves as floor is put up first. A light waterproof shelter is then built atop it.

Inquisitive bruins and grizzlies bring down an occasional cache. A precaution often taken in bear country, therefore, is to top one or more handy trees and use these to supplement the regular posts.

Tiny but hungry flying squirrels are pests in some localities, dropping to the towering storehouses from branches. The answer to this problem is to set the cache as much in the open as possible.

The casual forest dweller will not require a formidable cache. He will need storage facilities of some sort, however, be they but wire on which to hang blankets and a spring box in which to pack perishable foods in warm weather.

Wire

The cabin should afford means of storing bedding out of the reach of chipmunks and other diminutive denizens. Sufficient for ordinary needs is a wire stretched between two beams. Two parallel wires make a repository for sacks of flour and the like. Care will be exercised, of course, to store articles away from vantage spots from which small animals can drop or leap.

Chest

A metal-lined chest, perhaps built for auxiliary use as a bunk or window seat, can be particularly advantageous for the summer storing of winter paraphenalia. The lining may consist of fine screen, concealed if desired between two thicknesses of plywood. Sheet metal, particularly if soldered smoothly at all joints, is excellent, and many bushmen far from sources of supply take advantage of the handy flattened can.

Loft

Two or three poles set between purlins at one end of the cabin will form a general storage space. This can be of especial value in a winter-occupied northern cabin for keeping small supplies of canned milk and similar perishables safely above freezing floor temperatures.

32° F.

Foods frozen in the course of ordinary wilderness events should not be thawed until shortly before they are to be used. Texture and flavor of such fruits as oranges are best retained by defrosting them in cold water.

Frozen potatoes on the other hand may be skinned by scraping, then cooked immediately in constantly boiling water. They resemble marble in the frozen state. As to taste, sugar accumulates in potatoes stored in temperatures lower than forty degres Fahrenheit.

Fresh meat and fish keep excellently frozen. Eggs, cheese, fresh fruit, and vegetables are regularly preserved in the North by freezing although at impairment of flavor and quality.

A creditable trapper's stunt is to bake several dozen loaves of bread at a time, wrap each when cool separately in wax paper, and store the lot where all will freeze quickly. Brought in as needed and rapidly thawed in the oven, each loaf will be as fresh as if just delivered by a bakery boy.

Storage Cellar

"I dug my cellar in the side of a hill where a woodchuck had formerly dug his burrow, down through sumach and blackberry roots to a fine sand where potatoes would not freeze in any weather," noted Thoreau.

Some supplies burst their containers when frozen. Others are spoiled by frost. A ventilated pit beneath the cabin floor, described in Chapter Seven, usually proves a safeguard for such provisions. If there should be particularly large amounts of perishables to protect, a separate storage cellar may be the handiest answer to the problem.

Hills and knolls often ease the construction of a storage cellar which can then be scooped out of the slope without too much waste motion. Loam from above can later be slid down around any protruding wooden structure with a comparative minimum of effort.

The soil itself will serve as the walls if sufficiently firm. It is usually advisable, however, to set in at least corner posts to support roof timbers. Convenient shelves spiked between these will also serve as braces. Vegetable bins should be made of slats and kept in ventilated positions off the floor.

A substantial pole roof may be laid across the top of the cellar that is dug from the surface down. These poles should be protected by building paper or similar waterproofing although this precaution is not always taken. The roof can be insulated by a foot of dry browse overspread with several feet of dirt, preferably clay if that is handy.

A ventilator shaft will aid in regulating the temperature and humidity of the subterranean storage unit. Bushmen occasionally save old stove pipe for this purpose. A wooden flue can be put together in a few minutes, too. One six inches square will service a small cellar.

The ventilator should be screened. If necessary, a cap should be attached a few inches above the opening to keep out rain and snow. A lid should be handy for closing the vent in sub-freezing weather. During extremely severe spells in northern climes, the hole will also have to be stuffed with several feet of burlap sacks or paper.

The best entrance to the storage cellar is by means of two heavy doors, separated by a vestibule. These can be made on the spot by nailing together two layers of boards, one thickness laid vertically and the other horizontally, with insulative building paper between.

Waterproofing

Waterproofing is essential if any subterranean structure is to be relatively long lived. Only durable peeled sticks should be used for such construction. Heavy coatings of coal tar creosote or treatments with similar preservatives are necessary. Anyone going to the trouble of completing such construction will find it only sensible to protect his work by these and the other precautions described in detail in Chapter Three.

The use of heavy asphalt-impregnated roofing paper between the wooden roof and any non-waterproof covering is well advised insurance. In damp climates, an auxiliary water-tight roof some six inches above the dirt roof is well worth the extra effort.

Meat Tent

Surveying teams, hacking and perspiring their way through 'fly-infested bush, frequently pack along small meat tents. A common model consists of canopied netting with a zipper opening. The single top rope is fastened to a convenient branch in some shady, breezy spot. Here is kept everything from bacon to trout. A similar arrangement may be contrived with screen and light wooden framework for permanent use at the cabin.

Suspending Meat

Big game parties in the Rockies keep fresh meat sweet by suspending it, away from leaves and branches, upwards of twenty feet in the air. Here it is safe from blow flies.

Spring Box

Knock the bottom out of a wooden box and substitute two heavy slats. The spare boards may be used to close any cracks in the sides and to reinforce the lid which should be heavy for purposes of insulation.

Hinges for the lid may be improvised in several fashions nostalgic of covered wagon days. Bits of leather may be nailed into

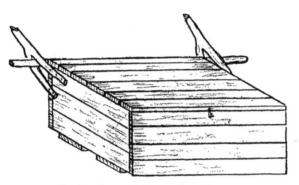

Spring box with wooden hinges.

place, or forked saplings may be angled over each end of a cross stick tacked to the lid.

Set the box, weighed down with several flat stones on the bottom, in the shady part of a stream. It is a good idea to keep such foods as butter in cans that will float safely in ordinary rises of water.

Barrel

An old barrel, partially buried a few feet downhill of a spring, often becomes a refrigerator of fame. Convenient pegs and shelves are soon installed. Cracks exposed to the air are chinked. Evergreen boughs spread over and around the barrel afford practical insulation.

Evaporation

Capillary attraction may be harnessed to provide bush refrigeration.

Build a box frame, one side of which is a hinged door. Put in several shelves of slats or poultry wire, making them as open as possible to encourage circulation. Then screen the box to assure its being fly proof.

Tack burlap over the contraption, lapping generously at door and leaving the top and bottom folds long and loose. A pan of water is placed on the top of the box, and the burlap ends are immersed in it.

Capillarity will keep the burlap saturated. If the box is set in a breezy spot, evaporation will do the cooling. Replenishing the water will be the only process not automatic.

Ice Chamber

"Wherever the ground is perpetually frozen and thaws out only a foot or so on top in summer, and where the nature of the terrain permits, any post can have a permanently frost-bound chamber underground," the Hudson's Bay Company advises its managers.

"Such an ice house or chamber is of the greatest value for the post mess, as it permits fresh meat, fish, birds, etc. to be stored and frozen whenever they are secured. These are then available for use as required throughout the summer months.

"Thus, many Arctic posts store a supply of deer meat in season which lasts them through the following summer. Fish and birds can be kept in the same way. In regard to keeping game birds in ice house, remove insides but do not pluck or the frost will dry them out.

"To build an ice chamber do this: Dig a small shaft three feet square and ten feet deep in the frozen ground. Excavate a chamber six feet high to the desired size. The roof of this chamber will then be four feet below the surface of the ground.

"A small frame, not over four feet high, is then built over the top of the shaft. This frame must have closely fitting double doors to give access to the shaft-head which itself will have double trap doors. The remainder of the frame is to be boxed in and covered over with earth, old coal sacks, etc., so as to insulate the entrance to the shaft.

"Fresh supplies may then be placed in the chamber at any time, and if the outside air (in summer) is properly excluded, they will be frozen solid in twenty-four hours and available for use whenever required, winter or summer."

Ice House

A small, tightly chinked log structure will serve as an ice house. If partially buried in a hill, the building will enjoy natural insulation and drainage.

The same principles of insulation, ventilation, and waterproofing discussed in connection with storage cellars are applicable to the ice house. Ice may well be removed at night to keep heat admission at the lowest possible minimum.

Two feet of sawdust between wall and ice is advisable. Additional sawdust should be used generously throughout, although such bush insulators as moss and grass may be substituted.

Ice

Some native may usually be delegated to fill the ice house if the owner is absent during the winter. Ice is most easily cut and handled when about eight inches thick.

Clean solid ice, less perishable than air-filled river cakes, may be manufactured during extremely cold spells by pouring water from nearby pump or spring into a large wooden form set in the middle of the frozen floor of the ice house.

This form is readily made of boards, cracks being sealed with wet snow. Newspapers will separate the ice into convenient eight-inch layers. If the cakes are reasonably well protected, one or two days of intermittent work during a really frigid spell will suffice for several years.

Ice House and Cache

A practical combination of ice house and cache may be built in a hogback or slope. The ice compartment can be buried except for a trapdoor in the roof. The cache, separated from it by a log wall in which a screened cold box is often set, can have a convenient horizontal entrance at ground level.

CHAPTER SEVENTEEN

HEAT AND LIGHT

An old wash tub overturned on a dirt floor, with a pot-covered hole in the top for wood and another opening for a rusty pipe, is the only stove in one prospector's cabin in the Rocky Mountains of British Columbia. Where materials are scarce and packs heavy, inventiveness thrives.

"You cheechakoos have too much to work with," this old timer, Bill Carter, grumbled to some builders at the King Gething mine in Hudson Hope recently. "When I joined the Mounted Police back in '98, all the equipment we got was a paper bag and a pointed stick. We used the bag for boiling tea. The stick was for killing game. And if you lost either one, son, you got charged with it."

Stove Pipe Alone

A trappers' favorite, because of the inexpensive ease with which a string of overnight cabins can be provided with warmth, is the heater made of stove pipe.

Join two sections of knock-down seven-inch pipe so as to make a single fourteen-inch cylinder. Unless the cabin already has a dirt floor, set this in a large box of sand or loam. Brace it with several rocks.

Four-inch pipe may be elbowed out of the top rear of the cylinder. Wire supports are generally improvised to steady this smoke vent.

A flattened section of pipe, bent at the edges so as to fit the top

227

of the stove more snugly, forms a lid that may be lifted for fuel-
ing. This is sometimes loosely hinged with wire or with metal
clips cut on the spot. An air hole is generally punched in the top.
Variations throughout, of course, are many.

Make four or more cuts with a can opener or ax, apple pie fashion, in the lower front of the cylinder. Push these flaps outward
to accommodate, for instance, a small baking powder tin open at
both ends. Care should be taken to clinch this can securely in
place. The lid of the small container can then control the draft.

Some bushwhackers use a cover punctured with nail holes for
medium draft, proving that one may revel in every comfort of
home by merely exercising the little grey cells.

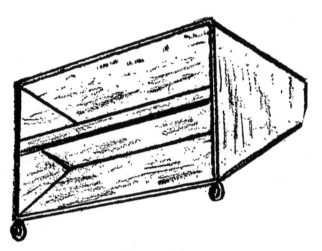

Reflector baker.

Cook Stove

The major requisite of the cook stove is that it have a well
functioning oven. A reflector baker set atop the stove can replace
this, it is true, but such a procedure is a nuisance at best.

If the oven door has no temperature gauge, one of the small
oven thermometers that sell for a few cents will be a particular
boon for the cook who is not accustomed to wood fires.

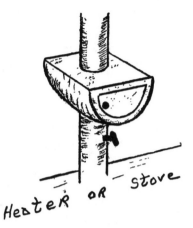

Drum oven.

Drum Ovens

Drum ovens, manufactured devices set in the stove pipe, will utilize for cooking purposes heat that otherwise would pass unhindered up the chimney. They are convenient for camps inasmuch as they permit use of the heater for both cooking and baking in cold weather when, otherwise, the kitchen stove might have to be lighted.

Drum ovens also harness escaping warmth. This is sole function of a similar device known commercially as a drum heater.

Pipe

The stove pipe, as pointed out earlier, should never touch wood or any other combustible substance. It should not pass within twelve inches, as a matter of fact, of such unprotected surfaces. This clearance may be safely lessened by the use of sheathing. The bushman sometimes adapts flattened tin cans for this purpose, showing once more what a self reliant man can accomplish with materials at hand.

Metal sheathing should be replaced when brightness becomes dulled if heat-reflecting efficiency is to be retained. If it is sound, however, one can refurbish it with aluminum paint. Some painstaking builders prefer the permanence and the conservative appearance of asbestos board.

Various types of stove pipe are on the market. It is good insurance, and usually smart economy as well, to obtain the most sturdy conductor available. Heavy galvanized iron pipe with tightly locked seams is excellent.

A species of pipe used much in the farther places is the interlocking black variety, sold in flattish rectangles of lightweight iron. Each snaps together to make a single section of pipe. Each of these narrows at one end and flares at the other so that the sections may be slipped firmly together to make a pipe of any length.

Finished pipe is so bulky and awkward that difficulties of transportation automatically rule out its use in many parts of the wilderness. A lot of frontier stores don't even stock it.

The home-joined pipe should be locked securely together according to the instructions received with it. One way to strengthen it further is by riveting as many sections to one another as practicable; using a hammer, a punch which may be nail, and some ordinary small copper rivets and washers. Thin black stove pipe corrodes quickly. It is a very good plan especially in the wilderness home to replace it yearly.

Home-Made Heater

Heaters made of metal gasoline drums stand up under roaring fires for decade after decade throughout the continent. The large billets they accommodate make them particularly advantageous.

There is often some cold-chisel artist in the locality back of beyond who will adapt such a drum for a few dollars. It can be made presentable enough, once completed, by applications of aluminum paint.

"All you need," says our friend, W. H. Carter, "is a gas barrel, a hammer and chisel, and a big chaw of tobacco."

The last time Bill converted one for me, however, he pressed several other widely assorted items into service as his own drawing shows. If the particular gadgets this ex-Mountie adapted hadn't been at hand, one can be certain that he would have nonchalantly substituted something else.

It's sort of like the case of the cook on a Canadian Geographi-

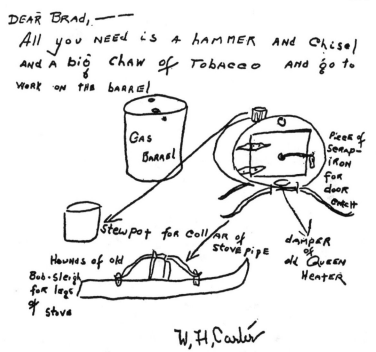

DEAR BRAD, ——

All you NEED is A HAMMER AND Chisel AND A big ChAW of TobAcco AND go to WoRK ON THE bARREl

GAS BARREl

PieCE of SCRAP- iRon foR dooR ＣＨＣＨ

Stewpot foR CollAR of STOVE PipE

damPER of old QUEEN HEATER

Hounds of old Bob-Sleigh foR legs of Stove

W, H, CarlEr

How to make an oil drum heater.

cal Survey party that Dr. W. H. McLearn of Ottawa took into the Peace River Block the other summer.

"Now where is that blasted, cussed, ding-danged . . . ?" Dr. McLearn (who's still wondering what he really ate that night,) heard this cook sputtering. "Oh, to blazes with it. This will do!"

Gas

Although wood and coal are the fuels most often used in wilderness homes, one is sometimes near enough civilization so that compressed gas may be available. If so, its advantage should certainly be considered.

So-called bottled gas, which is put out by a number of different companies, affords quick, hot, clean, and generally inexpensive warmth for cooking and for heating. Installations are rapidly and usually cheaply made, particularly when there is competition in the area. Tanks of gas are customarily delivered in pairs so that when one is empty, the other can be cut in until its mate is replaced. Permanent storage tanks are often furnished in locations which a tank truck can reach.

Circulator Heater

The circulator heater is a contrivance for warming the large wilderness home that has several rooms. It is a vest-pocket edition of the pipeless furnace described in Chapter Twenty-One. Not only does one afford better heat distribution than the ordinary type of heater, but the safety factor is increased inasmuch as the surface is comparatively cool.

Circulator heaters draw cold air from the vicinity of the floor, warm this air as it passes between casing and heated surface, and send it forth at the top to circulate through the house.

Precautions

Heaters should set on a fireproof base. When the firebox is close to the floor, a base that is made of sheet metal reinforced by quarter-inch asbestos sheeting will not be too drastic a precaution.

Heaters and stoves should be kept at least two feet from unprotected combustible surfaces. Metal reflectors may be used both to halve this distance safely and to radiate heat. Efficiency of these lessens as brightness diminishes. The reflector should be no less than one foot higher and wider than the heating unit.

Deodorant

Cooking odors may be pleasantly eradicated by dropping a small amount of evergreen pitch in one of the indentations provided for the lid lifter. Coffee grains do the job, too, when sprinkled atop the hot stove.

Conservation

The better the cabin is chinked and insulated, the easier it will be to heat. Banking the foundations and walls with earth and browse before frost sets in is an elementary precaution. Poles, laid horizontally, are often staked into place around the cabin to pen this temporary insulation.

Trail Stove

Two green logs laid in a pot-straddled V, with the larger opening toward the wind and with a fire kindled between, is all the stove needed on the trail. Two long strips of iron sometimes supplement the logs, as do grills. Convenient among the latter is the type, often home made, that folds like a pocket rule.

Here is the place for the reflector baker unless one is backpacking. The Dutch oven will be especially prized if its weight can be handled conveniently.

Puffers

If one heads into the rich northern Barren Lands where the tree line concludes abruptly, not thinning out gradually as one might suppose, a primus stove will be in order. These compact outfits, some weighing little more than one pound, may be secured in varieties burning alcohol, naphtha, kerosene, gasoline, benzine, seal oil, and other liquid fuels.

Light

The coal oil lamp is the old reliable of the bush. Sometimes surprisingly more profitable than thumbing mail order catalogues, however, is the exploring of unfashionable antique shops for these with the unvoiced awareness that rust can be removed from frames and bases and that ancient glass can be made to sparkle.

Wall and table models are generally preferable. A top-heavy effect is imposed on the small wilderness home by conversions of yokes and wheels. Such motifs, particularly if not given too rural a theme, better befit the large sporting lodge.

Artificial light occupies a more important position in the city than in the woods where, to get a fuller measure of life, one soon discards whenever possible regimented habits of late retiring and later rising. The experienced nomad steps back into wilderness routine by beating the sun up in the morning. Then getting to sleep early soon takes care of itself.

In the North, one of the numerous mantel or pressure lamps on the market is almost a necessity. Electricity, discussed in Chapter Twenty-One, is of course the most nearly perfect source of artificial light for every home.

Candles

Candles have the fluttering delicacy of the waning campfire. Holders vary from horizontal tin cans which protect the flame

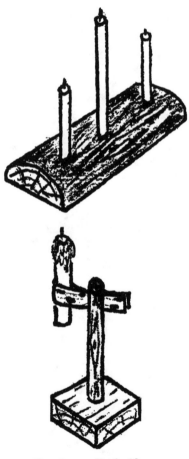

Rustic candle holders.

from the wind, the candle being shoved upward through a hole punched in the side, to rustic variations innumerable. One of the simpler of the latter is a cleft green stick securing a strip of birch bark which grasps the base of the taper. Another is the picturesque slab in which holes are bored or whittled. One risks severe damage to the eyes, however, by reading or doing exacting work by candlelight.

Elementals

Some bushwhackers turn to carbide and to alcohol for illumination. Other hard-bitten sourdoughs dump some animal oil in a can, drape an old bit of cloth over the edge for a wick, and give that the match.

CHAPTER EIGHTEEN

THROW ANOTHER LOG ON THE FIRE

Fireplaces have an undeniable charm. For what they consider good and sufficient reasons, however, few bushmen build them. Even the better fireplaces give little heat in proportion to fuel burned. They are generally drafty and, when not in use, cold. The building, furthermore, is arduous and exacting.

This is not intended to lessen enthusiasm for a fireplace, merely to point out its shortcomings. The good qualities are known to all.

While even the rankest greenhorn can put up a livable wilderness home, he may run into complexities if he proceeds further toward what some consider perfection. This stems to a certain extent from the fact that although the difficulties of cabin building are largely overestimated, the opposite is often the case with fireplaces.

The fact that *hearth* is synonymous with *home* in so many tongues is sufficient argument for a fireplace.

Franklin Stove

The simplest means of providing for an open fire in the wilderness home is by the use of the metal fireplace promoted by "Poor Richard" two centuries ago and still manufactured today. More effective than the built-in fireplace, the portable Franklin Stove radiates heat in all directions. A pipe is the only chimney needed.

Recirculation Units

A number of modified fireplace units are on the market. The better types are comparatively foolproof if installed with adequate chimneys. They already incorporate scientifically proportioned firebox, throat, smoke chamber, and other essentials.

These heavy metal forms are designed to be concealed by whatever masonry and woodwork the builder may prefer. They are usually accompanied by comprehensive instructions for installation.

When supplemented with a satisfactory chimney, a good unit will circulate heated air through several rooms. This is a definite improvement over the conventional fireplace whose performance on this score is practically non-existent.

Large quantities of heated air are still lost up the flue, however, a characteristic that prevents even the more expensive modified fireplace from approximating the efficiency of a good stove.

Foundation

Bed rock is the ideal foundation for the often incredible weight amassed in a fireplace and chimney.

A rugged concrete or masonry footing (a minimum twelve inches thick and at least six inches broader all around than the unit to be supported) is virtually a necessity, if only for reasons of safety and stability. It should be based in solid ground well below frost level.

The excavation for the foundation is most handily filled in many localities with large rocks set as firmly together as possible and bound with cement mortar flowed among them. These should be topped near the surface with a stone and cement slab at least a foot thick. Hearth, fireplace, and chimney can be constructed directly atop the slab, or if necessary this initial foundation can be heightened with additional masonry.

Reinforced concrete can be used in similar dimensions instead of masonry if there is a shortage of boulders. The procedure is the same as when concrete foundation piers are poured for the wilderness home itself, as described in Chapter Three. The general reinforcing in this instance, too, is accomplished by means of iron rods tied together at one-foot intervals with heavy wire.

When the slab alone is made of concrete, a reinforcement of heavy wire fencing, not less than eleven gauge, will strengthen it and guard against cracking.

Frost Level

The depth which frosts reach and heave varies so considerably that it should be ascertained locally. The frost level at magnificent Kluane Lake in the Yukon, where the Alaska Highway ribbons through Canada's highest mountains, is nine feet down. Permanently frozen soil is then contacted.

In many southern sections of the United States, on the other hand, there is never enough cold weather to freeze and thereby expand the moisture in the earth.

Mortar and Masonry

Mortar for fireplace and chimney use should not be proportionately leaner than one 94-pound bag of Portland cement, nine pounds of hydrated lime, and three times this combined volume of clean coarse sand.

Mixtures should be shoveled and hoed while dry until very thoroughly mixed. Only enough water should then be added to make a smoothly flowing paste, firm enough to support whatever masonry is being laid up.

Mortar and masonry, as well as concrete, have been particularized in Chapter Three. It may be worth repeating, however, that in hot dry weather all stones and previously completed masonry should be wet before fresh mortar is applied. In cold weather both should be dry and, if possible, warm.

Concrete

Concrete for use in fireplace foundations may well consist of one part of Portland cement by volume, two parts of clean coarse sand, and four parts of large screened gravel or crushed rock.

One part of Portland cement by volume can also be used with

six parts of unscreened gravel ranging in size from sand-like particles to pebbles.

Temporary wooden forms, well braced but lightly nailed so that they may be knocked apart easily, will facilitate construction of the fireplace footing. A double-headed nail that can be easily withdrawn is manufactured for this purpose. Smearing the forms with soap or grease will ease their removal.

Before or After

The best time to ready the fireplace base is when the cabin foundations themselves are being prepared. As a matter of fact, fireplace and chimney construction up to at least roof level is most advantageously completed at this period. It is easier, less wasteful, and far more tidy to build the home around this nucleus than to insert the unit bodily at some later date.

Cabin walls should not be built into the fireplace and chimney in any event. They may be handily provided for, however, by the laying of a groove in the masonry. In the case of stonework, this receptacle may be rough inasmuch as in all construction it will be expedient to plaster it with mortar to protect the wood against possible fire danger. Also for reasons of safety, it is better to project the groove rather than to indent it.

When the log ends are trimmed and fitted, a further advisable precaution is to keep them two inches away from all parts of the fireplace and chimney. The same clearance should be given the roof.

This space should be filled with some fire-resistant, flexible substance that will allow the masonry to move slightly without dragging the cabin out of line. Clay, mixed with water to the consistency of easily flowing paste, will serve. So will cinders if they happen to be at hand.

After

If the unit is to be added to an already standing cabin, the least destructive way to go about it will be to cut an opening in the wall just large enough to admit the fireplace proper. The bulk of this construction and the entire chimney can then be built outside the cabin.

The two cuts necessary in this instance can be made by a cross-cut saw after a keyhole saw, inserted through holes drilled by brace and bit, has been used to remove the top log in the opening. Boards to guide the blades should be nailed perpendicularly along the inside and outside of the wall with the assistance of a plumb line.

The wall should first be supported on each side of the proposed opening by being spiked to a pole or plank set solidly in the ground. These two stanchions may be located out of the way, two or three feet from the fireplace opening.

Stone

Most strong, sound varieties of stone in easily handled sizes will do for fireplace work. Stones high in quartz and other siliceous content, however, split and chip in heat. Stones from water beds should also be regarded with caution. Many contain moisture that, turned to steam by heat, causes explosions.

Some grades of sandstone are particularly adaptable. The flat slabs can be laid up swiftly and harmoniously. The richness of color inherent in many varieties lends a bright warmth to fireplaces, that too often revert to dark gloomy caverns when not in use.

If native fossil rock can be located in sufficiently hard types, a particularly interesting effect may be achieved by its use in decorative positions. The same is true of a number of petrified woods.

Semi precious stones such as jade, found in quantity along parts of the western side of the continent from Alaska through California, are possibilities both functional and picturesque when available in readily usable sizes. Jade's drawbacks for construction use, as a matter of fact, are its great weight and its toughness.

When the necessary stone is amassed, it should be graded for size, shape, quality, and color. The more ponderous pieces will be used closest to the ground, although some boulders may be fractured with a sledge to reveal fresh inner brightness. All unsightly sections and specimens will be hidden whenever possible.

Stones should be well bedded in mortar, heavily backed for security, and laid so that no vertical crack extends for more than one tier. All stonework in fireplaces and chimneys should be at least one foot thick.

Brick

Some will be prone to rule out brick for the wilderness fireplace on grounds that it is foreign to the frontier tradition. Yet ships sailing for Hudson Bay as early as 1685 carried brick and tile for fur trading posts in the New World!

Fire Brick

Fire brick is particularly functional for sheathing the inside of the firebox. The flickering flames are apt to crack and splinter native rock. The securest way to set these brick is flat with the long sides exposed.

Fire clay should be used whenever available for securing the fire brick. A rich cement mortar will do, however. Lime mortars are susceptible to disintegration by heat and gases and should be avoided in all fireplace work.

Jambs

The upright portions at each end of the firebox, known as the jambs, should not be too narrow for reasons of strength and sym-

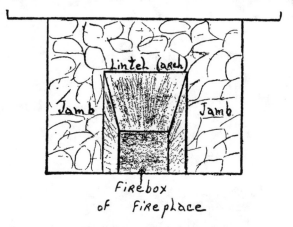

Front view of fireplace.

metry. An effective determinant is to make each jamb an inch or two wider than half of the fireplace opening.

There should be at least eight inches between the sides of the firebox and any combustible material. The latter should also be separated by two inches from any direct contact with the fireplace and chimney. A smoothly applied cement plaster will accomplish this.

Mantel

If there is to be a mantel (and more homes than might be expected could well do without what too often becomes an unsightly dust collector,) it may be supported by the jambs or by supports anchored in the masonry.

The mantel itself may be inserted in the stone or brick work. Here, too, all wood and other combustible materials should be

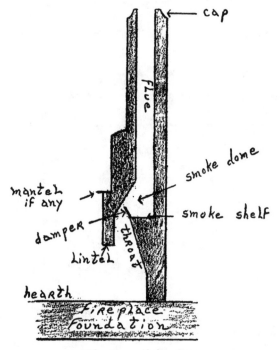

Side view of fireplace.

insulated with two inches of cement plaster from any direct contact with the masonry.

The wooden mantel, perhaps a split log or a venerable hewn timber, should be no closer than twelve or fifteen inches to the top of the firebox.

Hearth

The hearth may be a single magnificent slab or a cheerful conglomeration of flat or rounded stones. The first of these latter two will be easier to keep clean, particularly if the joints are left flush instead of being scratched out after the mortar has partially hardened.

Hearth and firebox may be elevated one or two feet above the floor to intensify heating effectiveness. This treatment is seen frequently in modernistic homes where it garners particular favor because of the way it agreeably places the blaze within ranges of vision that would otherwise be blocked by furniture.

This motif is not at all out of place in the most painstakingly authentic log cabin. The fireplace is stepped up in this fashion in the old Governor's Room at Lower Fort Garry in Canada, built in 1831 by Scottish stone masons where Winnipeg now stands. One in the ancient kitchen of the Hudson's Bay Company edifice is elevated by two steps. Both fireplaces have internal warming shelves where food may be set.

Specifications

Fireplaces five feet high and seven feet wide are in colonial tradition. Heights of from two to three feet are regarded as more practical, however, as the tendency to smoke becomes greater in proportion to height.

The more shallow the firebox, the greater will be the chance of smokiness. Although a deep opening radiates less heat, it compensates to an extent by accommodating chunks of wood that would otherwise have to be split. Danger from flying embers, too, is decreased.

If cordwood is to be burned, one should take into account the fact that such fuel runs four feet in length. The most practical way to adapt it is to saw it in half. These pieces will require an opening of from two and one-half to three feet wide.

Some architects specify that the width of the fireplace opening should be about one-sixth of the length of the wall in which it is set. Others stress that the total width of the fireplace construction should approximate one-third of the room's longest wall. Most agree that the final controlling factor should be the wilderness home itself. Toward this end, the two general rules are sometimes violated with dramatic and pleasing results.

Dimensions

The following table of fireplace dimensions scientifically compounded by the United States Department of Agriculture will take any guesswork out of internal designing.

Opening		Depth	Minimum back (horizontal)	Vertical back wall	Inclined back wall	Inside diameter round flue
Width	Height					
Inches	Inches	Inches	Inches	Inches	Inches	Inches
24	24	16-18	14	14	16	10
28	24	16-18	14	14	16	10
24	28	16-18	14	14	20	10
30	28	16-18	16	14	20	10
36	28	16-18	22	14	20	12
42	28	16-18	28	14	20	12
36	32	18-20	20	14	24	12
42	32	18-20	26	14	24	12
48	32	18-20	32	14	24	15
42	36	18-20	26	14	28	15
48	36	18-20	32	14	28	15
54	36	18-20	28	14	28	15
60	36	18-20	44	14	28	15
42	40	20-22	24	17	29	15
48	40	20-22	30	17	29	15
54	40	20-22	36	17	29	15
60	40	20-22	42	17	29	18
66	40	20-22	48	17	29	18
72	40	22-28	51	17	29	18

If a fireplace three feet wide is decided upon, for example, a glance at the table will show it should be thirty-two inches high.

The firebox may be from eighteen to twenty inches deep. The greater depth will have value in reducing the possibility of smokiness if, for instance, the house is among trees which may set up down-beating currents.

The next three columns in the table take into account the fact that, except for some direct radiation, fireplaces heat by reflection. The heat waves are bounced into the room from the sides and back of the firebox. So as to cast out as much warmth as possible, the sides of the firebox should slant inward toward the back. The back should slant forward after rising perpendicularly, in this instance for its first fourteen inches.

The final column indicates what size chimney opening is needed for the most thrifty and effective operation of the particular fireplace.

Arch

Although the well built masonry arch in the small fireplace will support itself, the neophyte will find it both easier and safer to employ a lintel bar. A flat or arched iron strip, one-half thick by three inches wide, will usually suffice. If the opening seems unusually wide, however, it will be inexpensive insurance to use two of these. The straight lintel bar will make subsequent masonry easier.

Most recirculation units and some commercial dampers themselves provide ample arch supports.

Throat

The throat is the narrowest part of the passage between the firebox and the smoke dome. The front and sides of the firebox lift to it perpendicularly, the back at a slant.

The throat should be at least eight inches above the lintel bottom no matter how large or small the fireplace may be. The throat's length should equal the width of the fireplace opening. Its area should at least be as large as that of the flue, a width of four inches generally serving excellently.

Damper

A damper should be installed at the top of the throat to regulate this opening so that the least possible heat will escape up the chimney. When a fire is not burning, it will usually be desirable to close this control entirely except when ventilation is desired.

A damper is a movable metal lid. It is hinged to a frame that is set in the masonry. The lid can be adjusted, usually by a handle, so as to increase or decrease the draft. If there is too much suction from the chimney, an unnecessarily high proportion of warmth vanishes uselessly up the flue. If there is too little draw, the fireplace will smoke. A roaring conflagration requires a larger throat opening than does a cherry-red bed of embers.

Smoke Shelf

The damper, which is hinged at the back and opens upward, also aids the smoke shelf in deflecting upward all downward moving gases. If this were not done, smoke would be driven into the room.

The smoke shelf is fashioned by connecting the back top of the throat horizontally across its entire length with the bottom rear of the smoke dome. The latter will be in line with the extreme back portion of the flue. The only requirement otherwise is that the smoke shelf be at least four inches wide.

Smoke Dome

The smoke dome, although some builders mistakenly omit it, is an integral part of the well functioning fireplace. It is here that smoke is imprisoned, instead of being blown into the room, when breezes puff down the chimney.

The smoke dome also gives continuously descending gases room in which to expand and thereby decrease their own speed. These errant currents course down the back of the flue to compensate for the partial vacuum caused by the rush of hot gases up the front of the chimney. The smoke dome brings them under control, then sees to it that they hit the smoke shelf at the proper angle to bounce upward and forward to mingle with the outpouring warm stream.

The smoke dome, that part of the fireplace bulging between throat and flue, is effected by slanting all but the perpendicular back wall upward and inward at thirty-three degree angles until the desired area of the flue is reached.

That is, for every three inches each wall rises, it slants inward two inches. The angle is determined easily enough with the aid of a square corner. That of a square-edged board or piece of paper will do. Measure two inches along the bottom of the corner. Measure three inches up the side. Then a line joining the two points will indicate the correct slant.

An easy way to construct the smoke dome is by drawing the front and side fireplace walls inward over a temporary wooden form which is subsequently disjointed and removed through the top.

All will then be in readiness for the chimney.

CHAPTER NINETEEN

SMOKE SOMETIMES RISES

If the builder becomes weary before the chimney is completed, he can always top it off with an old stovepipe. That is what Stewart Edward White did when building his wilderness home in the Sierras.

The combination seemed a bit ungainly at first, the outdoorsman admitted, but it drew like a furnace. He long enjoyed the illusion that one day he might extend the stones up over the pipe.

That's one of the joys of wilderness living, White pointed out delightedly. There are so many, many things that some day you can do.

The Chimney

Smoke curls upward, as anyone can testify who has gazed down on a New England hamlet from the banks of a trout stream some breathless Spring morning. A round flue offers the least resistance to this spiral action.

Evidence that a circular chimney opening leads the expanding and twisting fireplace gases upwards better than any other is emphasized by the fact that a flue with straight sides requires from one-fourth to one-third more area to do the same job.

The flue, which goes to prove that there is more to a chimney than can be seen, starts immediately above the smoke dome. Whether rectangular or circular, it should very definitely remain the same size throughout.

Correct flue dimensions, which are governed by the individual

248

fireplace, are tabled in the previous chapter. These measurements may be prudently increased somewhat if the cabin is closely surrounded by trees or is otherwise sheltered. It will be easier to close a damper slightly to offset a too powerful draw, than to set about increasing the suction by adding to the height of the ailing chimney.

Height

A chimney three feet taller than the loftiest portion of the roof will generally be high enough unless woods, hills, and other features setting up descending air currents make additional inches desirable.

Cap

Air currents will be swerved upward, increasing the desirable smoke-sucking partial vacuum, if the last few outer inches of the stone chimney are made to slope concavely inward until a four-inch mass is all that surrounds the flue.

Pebbles or gravel, used with the regular mortar, will do the job. Except for these final inches, the stone chimney should remain at least one foot thick throughout.

Brick chimneys, which are usually one block thick, are advisably capped for the additional purpose of reinforcing the top round against the loosening effect of wind and weather.

Cleaning

Another advantage the round flue had over the square is the comparative ease with which it can be effectively cleaned. This should be done, despite any momentary detriment to immaculate housekeeping, at least once a year. It is sound practice, in addition, to clean the chimney before starting a blaze in a cabin that has been deserted for some months. Covering the front of the fireplace with newspapers will help keep a fine black haze out of the rest of the home.

The most painless way to become a modern chimney sweep is by hauling up through the flue a burlap or cloth sack puffed with a soft yielding substance such as grass. The bag, which should fit with protesting tightness, can be affixed to a rope that has been lowered from the roof. More equal and therefore more effective pressure is maintained, of course, when the flue is round.

All flues should be periodically cleaned to remove any accumulation of foreign bodies such as leaves, to reduce the hazard of burning creosote, and to maintain a smooth surface that will afford the least possible resistance to ascending gases.

Lining

The use of a good commercial flue lining whenever practicable will lessen work and better assure a lastingly smooth surface.

Properly installed flue linings also minimize fire danger. Care should be taken for this reason to set all joints tightly and stoutly as a precaution against future leakage. This is particularly important when the chimney is built of a single thickness of bricks. Mortar is too often prone to loosen and crumble with age, opening crannies through which an otherwise unconfined ember can eventually and destructively dart.

Each section of the flue lining is locked to the next segment as the chimney rises. Each is firmly centered in cement with which the space between it and the rising chimney walls should be solidly filled. Any excess of mortar used for sealing joints should be wiped from the inside of the lining so as to leave a smooth, clean interior.

Concrete Alone

A piece of collapsible stove pipe can simplify the work of flue building for the wilderness dweller proceeding with a minimum of materials. If the correct circumference cannot be readily obtained, two such pipes can be riveted together on one side to make any size circle desired.

After the outer chimney stones have been laid to the height of the section of flue to be cast, the pipe should be centered and concrete poured around it. When the mixture has hardened, the pipe can be pressed inward and withdrawn for further use.

Two Flues

A flue should never have more than one inlet, but a chimney may have more than one flue. Each flue should be separated from every other flue by concrete or masonry at least four inches thick.

When flue lining is used as recommended, a further safety precaution is to stagger its joints throughout so that no juncture will be nearer than nine inches above or below any other junction.

Stovepipes

Any stovepipe leading into a chimney flue should be installed tightly by means of a thimble of metal, asbestos, terra cotta tile, or similar material. The pipe should extend no farther than flush with the inner circumference of the flue, so that the hot gases will be given full vent.

Such inlets may be provided for when the chimney is built by the use of a section of T-shaped flue lining manufactured expressly for that purpose. All such openings should be kept well sealed with a fire-resistant cap when not in use.

Runway

A cleated runway, long enough so that the pitch will be gradual, may be utilized for rolling rocks for the chimney into position.

Clearance

Although this provision is often neglected, careful builders prefer to allow a two-inch clearance between chimney and roof. This is done as a hedge against fire and against injurious expansion and contraction resulting from temperature fluctuations.

It is well to fill the space with some fireproof and yet flexible substance, so that even if the chimney moves slightly in heavy wind, no damage will result. Asbestos is excellent for this purpose. Pure clay, mixed with water so that it becomes a smoothly flowing paste, will serve. So will cinders.

Flashing

Flashing should be embedded in the masonry a few inches above where any portion of the chimney passes through the roof. The flashing should be covered by roofing material above and will cover that below. If there is any doubt as to whether or not this will make the junction waterproof, it will be expedient to

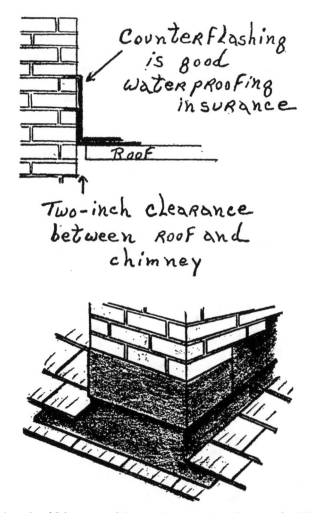

Counterflashing is good waterproofing insurance

Roof

Two-inch clearance between Roof and chimney

Flashing should be covered by roofing material above and will cover that below. Counterflashing is good insurance.

counterflash by setting additional flashing on the chimney several inches above the first.

The more permanent metals, such as lead and copper, will help to prevent later annoyance with leakage. If the source of supply is conveniently nearby, it may be advantageous to have the flashing cut from a single sheet. Otherwise, soldering is a good idea.

Wild Flux

Handy wilderness substitutes for solder are the tubes used for such products as toothpaste. Pitch from one of the evergreens such as spruce or fir will serve as flux.

Fittings

"The fittings of the fireplace, too, are worth notice," Stewart Edward White said in his nostaligic book, *The Cabin.* "When we built the chimney, we embedded in it a support for a crane. This was made of a piece of wagon tire. The crane was fashioned from the same material. From it depend old-fashioned pot-hooks and hangers, which are merely miscellaneous iron rods in disguise. Three utensils inhabit the fireplace: a heavy squat iron kettle, so ludicriously Dutch in build that we call it 'Gretchen'; and two iron pots. Every evening, even in summer, is cool enough for a fire. We do a great deal of cooking on that crane. It is exceedingly pleasant to hear Gretchen sing while the flames leap up the cavern of the chimney. . . .

"The 'fire-irons,' with one exception, are all homemade. Tongs are of tough oak steamed and bent double. The kettle lifter is an alder crook, appropriately cut and peeled. The poker is a piece of wild cherry, the handsome bark left on. The bellows is a small rubber tube with a few inches of flattened brass pipe inserted at one end; you blow into the other. The 'stand' is a fork of beautiful red manzanita, the ends of which are tacked either side one of the mantelpiece columns. But the fire shovel is the pride of the lot.

"That fire shovel is an example of the preciousness of treasure trove in the wilderness. A nail back of Shuteye is a marvellous thing. A tin can, whole and in good repair, becomes an invaluable coffee-pot. An abandoned dishpan is appropriated with a delight inconceivable. A chance piece of string rejoices the heart; and an old piece of paper is better than fine gold.

"So impressed is this truth on those who have travelled much away from civilization, that often a man becomes a sort of magpie in the collection of attractive things. . . .

"This spirit was responsible for our fire shovel. We discovered it, rusted, without a handle, bent and disreputable, in a heap of burned debris. It was one of those sheet-iron affairs with a fluted edge, that is ordinarily varnished black and in company with a coal skuttle. Why anybody brought it into the mountains in the first place would be difficult guessing. Anyhow, there it was. It 'looked valuable,' so we took it along. Now at last its being was justified. We knocked off the rust, straightened it out, fitted to it a beautiful white dogwood handle, and installed it in a position of honour. Now we point with pride to the fact that we are the only people in these mountains possessing a real fire shovel."

A Central Fireplace

The central fireplace of antiquity, superior in heating effectiveness to the usual recessed hearth, may be converted for log cabin use.

The simplest version is made by suspending a smoke trap, similar to that used by a blacksmith, over a blaze kindled on a dirt floor. A stovepipe will be all the vent needed for this metal canopy.

A well sheathed box, filled with at least a foot of sand or other non-combustible material can be used to protect a wooden floor. Masonry will, of course, be better. A four-sided fire screen should be improvised to guard against sparks.

Massive stone pillars and an imposing rock chimney will make the central fireplace as pretentious as the most classically minded may desire.

A Hood Fireplace

A very effective shallow fireplace can be constructed against fire-resistant masonry with a metal hood taking the place of jambs, front, and mantel. A fireplace of this sort will bulge comfortably from a corner of a small room or cozily hug a long wall.

Some such fireplaces are built one or two steps higher than the floor. Many of the smaller are designed to accommodate logs set upright.

The motif is very definitely functional as well as striking, inasmuch as the metal hood radiates heat.

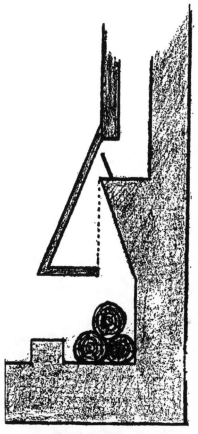

Hood fireplace.

Fireplaces are constructed along similar lines with masonry alone. The adobe fireplace of the Southwest is an example. Without a hood of burnished copper or some similar metal, of course, these lack the radiant feature.

A Clay Fireplace

Common in some parts of the continent is the fireplace in which log frames, set outside the house, are lined with clay-covered stones or with foot-thick clay.

Such a fireplace should be built on a rock-filled pit extending below frost level. A temporary wooden form, behind which wet clay can be packed and pounded, will help to assure a neat job. Any frontal woodwork in danger of being charred should be sheathed with metal.

Clay Chimney

A protective air space between clay chimney and cabin wall, with sturdy anchorage at the roof line, is recommended.

The chimney may be picturesquely made of small peeled sticks, notched into place log cabin style. These should be well plastered inside and out. A piece of stovepipe, used as suggested earlier in this chapter, will simplify the moulding of the flue.

Clay fireplaces and chimneys have been successfully used for year after year, but even the more carefully constructed should be kept in unquestionable repair to minimize fire danger as much as possible. Except in instances where a fireplace is a necessity and no other kind is practicable, the clay version should usually be avoided.

Flue Testing

Flues should be stringently tested for possible leakage before being used. It is a sound practice to test them at least annually thereafter. Any leaks should of course be located and repaired without delay.

A satisfactory test takes very little time. One builds a small, quick fire of some smoke-producing substance in the fireplace. A few scraps of tarred building paper will do the job at the touch of a match. The chimney top is covered with sodden newspapers or a wet canvas. The thus trapped smoke will soon reveal any cracks or crevices in the flue structure.

Covering

Flues should be covered when the wilderness home is vacated so as to exclude foliage, moisture, dust, and feathered and furred adventurers. The woodsman's choice for topping his creaking stovepipe is often an old bucket or rusty lard pail.

A wooden cap that can be drawn over a chimney may be nailed

together in a few minutes. It is not a bad idea when building to embed several protruding nails in the last foot of the chimney so that a cap may be fastened on securely with wire. String or rope should not be substituted for metal as long as squirrels and other thrifty wildfolk have appetites, teeth or beaks, and brave curiosity.

The Dutch Oven

The genuine Dutch oven, although built in the masonry of the regular fireplace and heated by hot coals from that fire, is actually a miniature fireplace in itself. It requires a separate damper, flue, etc.

Dutch Oven.

The portable Dutch oven is a simpler substitute. Choice among these is the heavy, old fashioned, cast iron utensil. One may bake or roast in a fireplace with one by embedding it in live coals, then covering it with heat-retaining ashes. Supper may thus be started in the morning and without further attention will be deliciously hot by evening, flavor and juices intact.

Ted Boynton, who cooked for big-game parties from the Cassiars to the Barren Lands, always packed along his own personal Dutch oven. It was so large that he once curled a whole cub bear inside with enough vegetables to satisfy a hungry outfit of eight.

Outdoor Fireplaces

Outdoor cooking facilities are convenient when visitors over-flow, when it's desirable to keep the cabin cool in hot weather, and when one just plain wants to get outdoors.

Nothing elaborate nor expensive is needed. A very satisfactory outdoor fireplace may be built in a few hours with cement, sand,

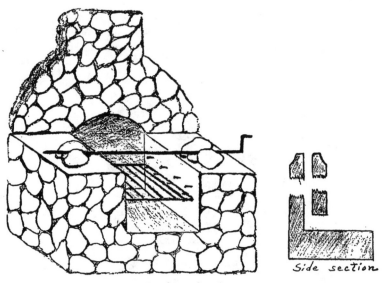

Side section

Outdoor fireplace.

stones or bricks, and some metallic odds and ends that when not already at hand may be improvised from the contents of almost any junkyard or second-hand store.

Design is optional, but the following details are worth consider-ing. A raised firebox, which for ordinary cooking purposes need not be over fifteen inches wide, will lessen stooping.

Use of a grate will reduce the blaze more speedily to the de-sirable hotly glowing coals recommended in Chapter Twenty-Three. Almost any heavy open metalwork will do for a grate. It may be stood on bricks so that the firebox can be easily cleaned.

Several series of spikes embedded on each side of the firebox walls will permit the setting of an iron grill at different levels above the heat.

A simple chimney will make for better draft and less troublesome smoke. Straight lines are all that will be necessary. The chimney details called for when an indoor fireplace is built are not needed in the open air.

A removable iron rod, set in masonry sockets, will serve as a handy spit for those who occasionally like to do their roasting and barbecueing in the great out doors.

Great Out Doors

What could be more appropriate than the fact that the initials of these three words spell GOD!

"You have spoken well," Warburton Pyke, the northern explorer, tells of a native saying to a missionary. "You have told me that Heaven is very beautiful. Tell me one thing more. Is it more beautiful than the country of the musk ox in summer when, sometimes, the mist blows over the lakes? And sometimes the water is blue, and loons cry very often. . . .

"That is beautiful. If Heaven is still more beautiful, my heart will be glad, and I shall be content to rest there till I am very old."

CHAPTER TWENTY

OUTDOOR LIVING

"My best room, always ready for company, was the pine wood behind my house," Thoreau said. "Thither in summer days when distinguished guests came, I took them. And a priceless domestic swept the floor and dusted the furniture and kept the things in order."

Bridges, fences, dams, corrals, bird shelters, dog houses, and log turnstiles all may enhance one's pleasure beneath nature's jade-cool trees, serene blue sky, and tawny sunshine.

Fences

Fences are necessities for some backwoods homes especially where livestock ranges, where deer raid gardens, and where hungry sled dogs steal everything from soap to leather book covers.

Cedar, juniper, redwood, cypress, osage orange, chestnut, iron oak, locust, and similar durable woods are preferable for posts, as they resist ground decay. It is well to treat with preservatives all wood that is to come in contact with the ground. This may be inexpensively and quickly accomplished by brushing on heated coal tar creosote. Or one of the other procedures indicated in the index may be followed.

Rustic fences of varying degrees of ingenuity have a popularity longer lived when designs follow simple lines instead of the garish and gnarled fopperies too often sought.

A plain pole fence can be made by driving pairs of sticks into the ground at opposite angles, wiring or nailing them where they

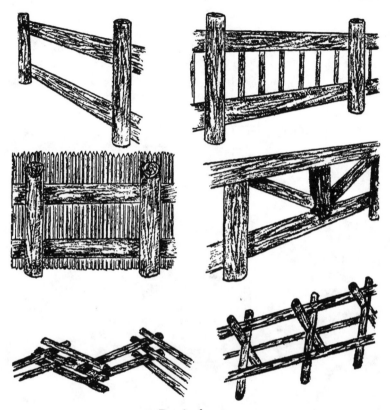

Rustic fences.

cross, and laying poles in the crotches. One or more additional rails may be secured to the uprights.

The split rail fence of Honest Abe's day still zigzags its way over many a countryside, although the ease with which one is laid up with the horizontals supporting one another is overweighed by the task of riving these.

Slabs nailed to a frame made by attaching top and bottom poles horizontally to ground-embedded posts make an inexpensive rural fence for enclosing garden patches in rabbit country. Cutting off the exposed tops of such posts at an angle will help prevent water from seeping into the grain.

Palisades

Palisades have long been a part of the wilderness picture. Wiring or spiking the long and traditionally sharpened poles to upper and lower crosspieces, fastened horizontally between posts, makes a more permanent job than the old procedure of basing each in the ground.

Indians brought pickets twenty-two feet long and about three

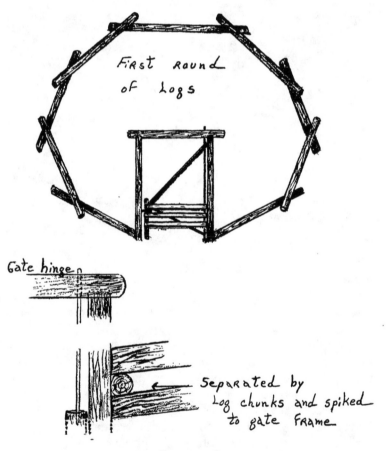

Log corral.

feet in circumference to Fort Victoria when that present British Columbia capital was built on Vancouver Island in 1843. For every forty pickets of that size, the Scotsman superintending the construction for the Hudson's Bay Company thriftily paid one blanket.

Corral

A handsome corral, which will enhance the swankiest wilderness estate, is one of the simplest log structures to build as the picture shows. The joints, which may be made by rough saddle or lock notches, should be ruggedly spiked, pinned, or wired. Although size is optional, the more massive the logs are, the more striking will be the result.

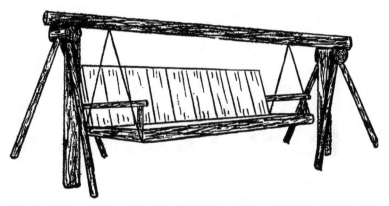

Rustic swing, with pole tripods such as those used by Mackenzie River Indians.

Outdoor Furniture

Outdoor furniture, several types of which are mentioned in the general chapter on the subject, can increase one's enjoyment of natural surroundings. As Thoreau noted, "None is so poor that he need sit on a pumpkin. That is shiftlessness."

The illustrated settle may fit into some nook. The back is so pinned that it can be swung down for use as a table, in which case a foot rest in front will become a bench.

Settle.

Turnstile

A turnstile—which need be but a four-armed cross of poles, bored in the center so that it will turn on a spike or peg set in the top of a post—will be more convenient than a gate in some instances, as between wood lot and cabin.

Dog House

Any number of log cabin effects may be incorporated in a dog house. If the pet is to be comfortable, his home should be dry and well ventilated. Most important of all, a sleeping platform should be added so that he may curl up out of drafts. The dog will appreciate bedding, particularly some old clothing long worn by his master. Whatever the bedding is, it should be kept aired and clean.

Bridge

Several poles, tops flattened and bottoms held together at two or three intervals by well spiked crosspieces, make a satisfactory bridge for spanning a small coulee or brook. Effective, too, is the nailing of sound slabs at right angles across the tops of two naturally arched logs. The footing, whatever it is, should be smooth.

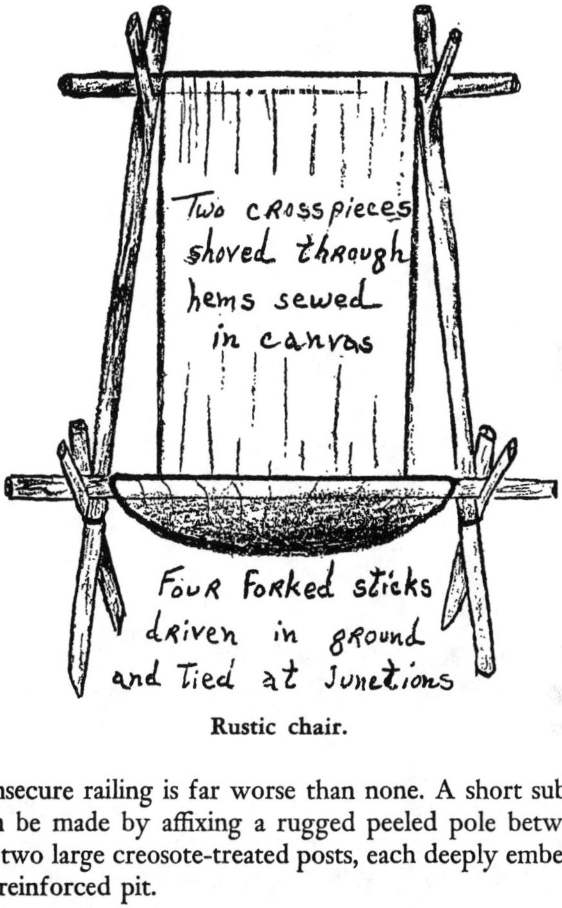

Two crosspieces
shoved through
hems sewed
in canvas

Four Forked sticks
driven in ground
and Tied at Junctions

Rustic chair.

An insecure railing is far worse than none. A short substantial one can be made by affixing a rugged peeled pole between the tops of two large creosote-treated posts, each deeply embedded in a rock-reinforced pit.

Dam

Many a wilderness brook clamors musically for a low dam behind which to pause, meditate, and incidentally provide a pool for washing. A simple enough barrier can usually be made by piling rocks across a narrow stretch.

A wooden peg driven into a tree—in a hole made by a spike, gimlet, or more primitively by an ax gash—will furnish a point on which to hang a toothbrush if no twig is handy. Four pegs, driven at angles into two trees, will support a rustic towel bar.

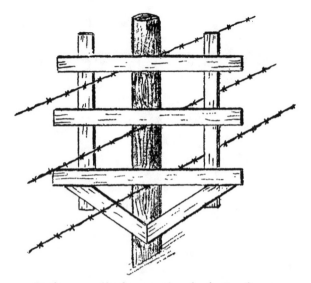

Stationary stile for crossing barbwire fence.

Rod Holder

For temporarily storing rigged fishing rods readily and safely, bore in a short pole a number of inch-deep holes large enough to accommodate the butts. A little whittling will give these cavities a hand-fashioned look.

Nail or peg the stick in a protected spot under the eaves on the cabin wall. Fasten above it a slotted pole of similar dimensions. Pivoting sticks, turning over the respective slots, will handily lock in the Shakespeares, Bristols, Heddons, and True Tempers.

Vane

A vane is of practical value to both sportsman and to weather prognosticator. Some member of the party should be sufficiently versed in the departing art of whittling to turn a shake into a creditable salmon or goose.

The vane, which should twirl freely, should be installed where it will not be deflected by misleading air currents. Marking the compass points simply beneath will aid strangers in becoming oriented.

Names

The day will come when the wilderness dweller will be seized with the desire to burn in a hewn slab or spell with gnarled wood the name of his forest haven. Let him be forewarned. The Red Gods who dwell in the cabin eaves, protecting those who enter invited beneath the roof, are said to slink away from log cabins desecrated by such debilities as Bide-a-Wee and Dewdrop Inn.

Mail Box

If the cabin owner chances to be where a mail box is necessary, he may find it fun to build one in the exact model of his wilderness home. An end can be hinged, or the whole roof can be made to swing open. The miniature may be mounted on a post to which, perhaps, the name of the family is also attached.

Bird Shelters

"I found myself suddenly neighbor to the birds, not by having imprisoned one but having caged myself near them," Thoreau observed.

Bird shelters built of such rustic materials as slabs, shakes, and hollowed logs will not only benefit feathered life, but they will afford endless pleasure to the wilderness dweller who is invading their sanctuary. The house should be reasonably waterproof, cool, and accessible for observation and seasonal cleaning.

Such supports as poles or small trees should be made impassable by metal sheathing for about eighteen inches above any points that predators such as squirrels and cats can reach by jumping or climbing.

House types vary in bird land, too. Four slabs selected from the woodpile, two ends sawed from a small log, several nails, a bit of leather for a top hinge, and about fifteen minutes will make the picturesque model illustrated. A peg may be driven beneath the whittled entrance for a perch.

The same materials may be utilized to provide a feeding station. Its storage compartment, reached by a flap, may be kept filled with crumbs and scraps that gravity will shift under the open front to the feeding ledge.

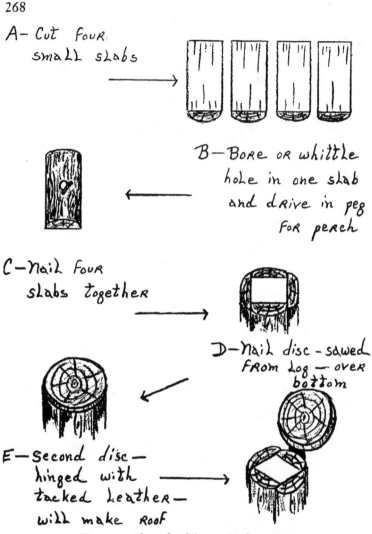

A— Cut FouR small slabs

B— BoRe or whittle hole in one slab and drive in peg FoR perch

C— Nail FouR slabs togetheR

D— Nail disc - sawed FRom log — oveR bottom

E— Second disc — hinged with tacked leatheR — will make Roof

How to make a bird house in five steps.

Birds, like mosquitoes, can get in through mighty small openings. A one-inch entry will make any wren happy, while the nuthatch demands an additional quarter-inch. Tree swallows, chickadees, and bluebirds are pleased with inch-and-a-half doors to their cabins. The red-headed woodpecker won't play house unless accorded two inches.

Martins will dwell in colonies but not unless the front gates have two-and-one-half-inch diameters. The little grey owl with the big screech prefers a three-inch portal, while the church owl solemnly prays for at least a half-foot circle.

Totem-Pole

One with an artistic turn of hand may be able to incorporate in the crude charm of a totem pole the history of camp, hunt, and family.

Coast Indians in the Northwest, who fashioned everything from cooking utensils to clothing from the cedar tree, used this wood for their heraldic poles. Their totems served as coats of arms, sign boards, and symbols of rank. Some were so huge that a hole in the base formed the cabin entrance. Totem poles were also sometimes used inside the house as roof supports.

The aborigines carved and painted such creatures as the bear, wolf, mountain goat, raven, owl, eagle, beaver, frog, and hawk. Paint was made from such materials as colored earths, burnt bones, and pressed berries. Tools were of stone, shell, and bone, while Russians supplied a few rude iron knives in the seventeen hundreds.

Modern inventiveness can be armed with axes, chisels, fine steel knives, and other tools ranging from the tiniest of saws to the largest of planes.

Stairs

An outdoor type advantageous in snow country consists of two inclined poles covered with cleated slats. A few strokes of a broom can then clear away the effects of a blizzard. As the High Lama of Shangri-La noted, "Laziness in doing stupid things can be a great virtue."

CHAPTER TWENTY-ONE

MODERN AS TOMORROW

The wilderness home may be located back of beyond, but that does not mean it cannot be as modern as today's news bulletins. The very wind can be harnessed to provide electricity. Such popular conveniences as refrigerators and washing machines will operate on coal oil or kerosene. The individual has only to decide how many time-and-work-savers he can install before they themselves become burdens.

"We do not go to the woods to rough it; we go to smooth it— we get it rough enough in town," a philosophic woodsman named Nessmuk pointed out three-quarters of a century ago. "But let us live the simple, natural life in the woods and leave all frills behind."

Water

Convenient water sources higher than the cabin may be piped into the forest home with gravity's taking the place of a pump.

Purity of any supply is necessarily of prime importance. Streams that natives assert are pure are not necessarily so. Before any source is adopted for use, the water should be determined safe by reliable scientific judgment. Tests are performed free by numerous health boards and universities, many of whom even provide sterilized sample jars without charge. If results are favorable, the examinations should be repeated at regular intervals.

Purifying

Doubtful water, to be purified by heat, should be boiled at least twenty minutes. A pinch of salt will improve the taste somewhat if one finds it flat. The actual cause of this insipidness, however, is loss of air. This can be partially restored on a small scale by shaking the sterilized drinking water in a partly filled container.

Water can be disinfected chemically although such methods, to be absolutely safe, should be based on chemical analysis of the particular water. Such foreign substances as silt, iron, and nitrates cause germicidal actions to vary.

P-sulfonedichloramidobenzoic acid, marketed at drug and sporting goods stores under the more pronouncable name of Halazone tablets, is a safeguard particularly handy for carrying in the pocket. So are so-called chlorine tablets. Both should be used according to directions on the containers.

A disinfectant for home use may be prepared by dissolving one teaspoon of fresh chlorinated lime in one quart of water. One-half a teaspoon of this solution will usually purify one gallon of water in half an hour. The stock solution should be kept in a tightly corked bottle marked, "Poison." Fresh solutions should be made up periodically, as strength is gradually lost.

Tincture of iodine is also an emergency water disinfectant. The fresh tincture ordinarily contains about seven per cent iodine. One drop of this tincture mixed thoroughly with one quart of water will generally make the latter fit for drinking in a half-hour.

Sweeten

Ill-smelling water may often be sweetened, as well as rid of germs, by boiling it for twenty minutes with some charred wood. It is then skimmed and either strained or allowed to settle.

Filter

A wilderness filter may be made, particularly in sandy soil, by digging a hole several feet from the source of supply and using the water that seeps into it. Filtering, however, neither materially affects dissolved mineral content, nor does it guarantee purity.

Water is polluted by animal and mineral matter, incidentally, rather than by decaying vegetable substances.

Softening

Water may be satisfactorily softened for washing purposes by the addition of borax, sal soda, or ammonia. Drinking water may also be softened, either by boiling or by use of one of the several manufactured devices on the market. First, however, analysis should be made to determine what carbonates, sulphates, chlorides, or other hardening constituents are present.

Pumps

Hydraulic rams, which pump automatically by self-variation of water pressure, are not surpassed in economy in the pump field. The current of a small brook or even the overflow of a spring is often enough to operate such a ram. Combination rams may be harnessed to brook power for the pumping of spring water.

A suction pump will satisfactorily lift water about twenty-one feet when used at sea level and approximately one foot less for each additional thousand feet of elevation.

Force pumps, together with combination force-and-suction pumps, are also used in the woods. They may be obtained for operation by electrical, gasoline, oil, water, hot air, and wind power.

Water may be pumped as needed, in which case the old fashioned suction pump that is worked with a handle may as well be installed. It may also be stored in wood, masonry, or metal tanks elevated above all outlets. Pressure (air on water) tanks will do away with any need for altitude.

Wells

It will usually be possible to locate the wilderness home beside a satisfactory water supply. Occasionally, however, a well will have to be dug or driven. Both procedures entail unfortunate amounts of perspiration. Unless one has had some experience, it is therefore not a bad idea to recruit a neighbor whose knowledge of the locality will increase the chances of striking an adequate supply of good water at a reasonable depth.

A driven well is made by hammering a pipe into the ground until a satisfactory body of water is penetrated. A particularly rugged wrought-iron pipe, with a diameter of some two or three inches, is generally used. This is tipped with a steel pointed section of pipe whose sides are lined with copper-screened holes.

The other end of the pipe is temporarily covered with a special cap which protects it from the blows of maul or sledge. When one section of pipe is buried, another is joined to it and the work continued. A well may be driven down 75 or 100 feet by hand, although depths even approaching this extreme are seldom necessary or advisable for a wilderness home.

When a well is driven in the wilderness, it's more often to discover water than to serve as a permanent fixture. The trouble with driven wells is that the points have a tendency to clog. These holes may be cleared for awhile at least by forcing water down the pipe with a hand pump. Time and trouble may often be saved in the long run by testing until water is reached within some twenty feet, then digging.

It takes two men to dig anything but a very shallow well. One of these should very assuredly have enough experience to guard against possible cave-ins. The dirt may be raised hand over hand by a rope and pail. It is more workmanlike to use a block and tackle suspended over the excavation from a tripod made by tying the tops of three poles together as described in Chapter Seven.

Dug wells should be lined along their upper portions with masonry or tile if possible, although wood is more often used for this purpose along the frontier. A fast and effective job can be done by walling the lower part of the well with loose rock, then finishing it off with large concrete or tile pipe installed with the large ends up and with the joints bedded in mortar.

The last four feet or so of the well lining should be made watertight so that surface moisture will not leak directly into the drinking supply. It is advisable to fill in around this final stretch with concrete. or clay for this reason and to extend the casing safely above the surface of the ground, capping it tightly with a wooden or cement cover.

It cannot be emphasized too strongly that every effort should be made to keep any water supply free from contamination. Since underground conditions that cannot be seen may sometimes thwart every precaution at some times of the year, as when levels become abnormally low in dry weather or unusually high in the springtime, it is no more than good common sense to have the well water tested regularly.

Pipes

Pipes may be concealed in slabbed logs that are later screwed together for easy access. They may also be hidden in chinking. Convenient drain cocks should be located so that all parts of the system can be emptied if this must be done to prevent freezing. Traps should then be left filled with a liquid anti freeze which in the bush may be ordinary coal oil or kerosene.

It is well to have the water analyzed before pipe is purchased. Different metals are more or less affected by otherwise unobjectionable chemicals present in various water supplies. No one type of metal pipe is made that will withstand the corrosive effects of every sort of good drinking water.

Copper tubing is more resistant than most, however. It has other definite advantages for log cabin use, not the least of which is the fact that it comes in easily transported rolls.

Exact measurements are not necessary with copper tubing. If a section is cut too long, it is an easy matter to curve it slightly to make it fit. Copper tubing can easily be bent around corners and obstructions without a lot of complicated cutting, threading, and coupling.

The lightweight soft-brown product is generally the most suitable of the copper tubings for the wilderness home. The fact that this will expand sufficiently to withstand several freezings without bursting adds a safety factor to its other recommendations.

Whereas a pipe vise, cutter, reamer, die, and special wrenches have to be used to install iron and other solid pipe, copper tubing can be connected either by soldering or by simple use of flared fittings. The tube is cut by an ordinary hacksaw in this latter instance. A nut is slipped loosely on. A flaring tool is then inserted in the tube and tapped with a hammer to expand the end so that it will tightly hold the nut which is then screwed securely into the fitting.

Hot Water

Hot water can be made available by installing coils in a stove, heater, or fireplace. A supply of running water is not even a necessity.

A hot water tank may be improvised from the same type of gasoline drum that makes so excellent a heater. The simplest thing to do with this metal barrel is to cut out its solid end with a hammer

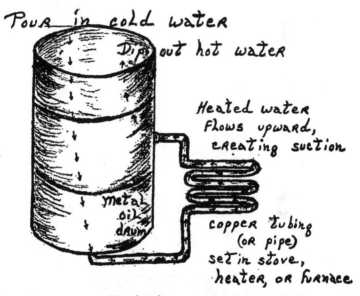

Simplest hot water system.

and cold chisel. The receptacle may then be set on a substantial wooden base, about a foot high, near the cook stove.

A coil is easily fashioned of sections of one-inch pipe elbowed into loops that will fit into the front of the stove. One end of this loop is connected to the bottom of the drum where a threaded opening awaits it. The other end is piped to a second threaded hole already in the middle side of the metal barrel.

Water is poured through the open top of the drum. Heat causes it to circulate. Hot water, being lighter than cold, keeps rising upward from the higher pipe and can be dipped out as needed. This causes a vacuum that results in the lower pipe's sucking in more of the cooler water, and so on.

The principle remains the same no matter how expensive a system is installed.

Electricity

Windmills, water wheels, and variously fueled motors produce electricity for direct use and for storage in batteries. Compact generators, driven by tiny gasoline motors, are surprisingly inexpensive to buy and operate. A small DC outfit will be sufficient to operate several strategically placed bulbs at a time, as well as a radio.

Wiring, particularly for the small low powered units, is easily and safely done. Instructions usually come with each generator, or they may be obtained from the dealer. It is simple enough to conceal wiring between logs, in chinking, beneath the floor, or atop beams. Fixtures should be kept as plain as possible, aesthetically speaking, so as not to distract from the rustic atmosphere. Shades with woodland scenes are often effective.

Heat

A cellar with twelve square feet of floor space, its height depending on the furnace, will accommodate most small heating systems together with a fuel supply if one wants something more than ordinary stoves and heaters. Wood will usually suffice for the fuel. Coal outcrops in some sections recommend that combustible, however, as do transportation difficulties in regions such as the treeless leagues along the Arctic Ocean.

Warm air systems are better suited to the bush than types based on hot water and steam. Principal reasons for this are comparative ease and inexpensiveness of installation, quick response to regulation, and the absence of danger of damage by freezing.

The so-called pipeless model, essentially a stove encased in a metal shell, performs well. This is a large edition of the circulator heater described in Chapter Seventeen. Cold air drawn from the house is warmed by passing between casing and heated surface. Dispatched through a centrally located radiator, it goes through the home to return upon cooling. Units are usually accompanied by directions that enable the home owner of ordinary handiness to assemble them easily and effectively.

Primitive

"It is some advantage to lead a primitive life if only to learn what are the gross necessities," said Thoreau over a century ago. "Most of the luxuries, and many of the so-called comforts of life, are not only not indispensable but positive hindrances. Our life is frittered away by detail."

CHAPTER TWENTY-TWO

SUSTENANCE IN THE SILENT PLACES

The bush cook, meagre though his materials may be, has one tremendous advantage over the most lavishly equipped city chef. The latter too often has to stimulate the small appetites of dyspeptics. The pot-and-pan man of the wilderness has hearty hunger for an ally.

Cooking Fire

The main fault of the novice outdoor cook is that he doesn't know the difference between a bonfire and a cooking fire.

"Cheechakoos figure they've got to cook aitch-for-leather," explains Ted Boynton, famous northwestern trail cook. "That ain't speed. It's just a handy way to burn the grub and likely yourself.

"The idea is not to cook over flames. Glowing red coals are the best. You sure wouldn't need a forest fire, anyway. If it's cold, build a separate fire of warmth. Why, I can wrangle a whole meal with no more wood than I can carry in this here hat."

Skillet Substitutes

The white man's frying pan has ruined more Indians than fire water. This cooking weapon should be used sparingly, particularly when loaded with grease.

The flashiest outfit Ted Boynton ever hoisted a Dutch oven for was the Charles F. Bedaux expedition. Bedaux (at whose French chateau Wallis Simpson and the Duke of Windsor were married) had crossed the African deserts with five passenger cars. He es-

278

timated it would be an easy matter to ride tractors through the Canadian Rockies.

Bedaux set out with five tractors, 130 horses loaded largely with gasoline, and enough kitchen paraphernalia to outfit a Palm Springs hotel.

"Why now, if I'd ever tied into all them fancy kettles and such, I never would have got anything done," Ted admits. "Bedaux didn't give an aitch, though. So in my spare time, I showed him how small an outfit a bush cook can get along with."

Ted taught the internationally renowned efficiency expert how to grill venison steaks by sandwiching them between two hot stones. Ted showed him how to ribbon bread dough around a heated green stick, then brown it over hot embers.

Bedaux was most interested, though, in the way Ted split some Arctic graylings up the back, then pegged them flesh-side-out on heated birch slabs. These Ted leaned close to the fire, occasionally turning them end for end. When the fish became flaky, individual hot plates were all attached.

"Did Bedaux get through the mountains with his tractors? Nope," says Ted, "he lost just about his whole outfit. But he sure learned how to plank a fish."

Mud Hen

The rotund cook had one of his hardest workouts when he went up into unexplored Northwest Territory and Yukon regions with Harry Snyder, prominent in developing Canadian uranium deposits. Then American Museum of Natural History scientists, who took pictures of musk ox and gathered hundreds of museum specimens, had Ted cooking all the wild edibles he could find.

The numerous varieties of wild onions, Ted Boynton showed them, pep up any salad. Rock tripe is good for thickening soups. So are ordinary blue violets. Young birch twigs make a pleasant tasting tea. The dried leaves of the ground cranberry, mixed with tobacco, make a pungent smoke that some Northerners have grown to prefer to pure tobacco.

"I guess they reckoned they had me stopped proper, though, the day they lugged in a brace of mud hens," Ted chuckles. "I remember how Mr. Snyder allowed he'd tried mud hen before.

He said that if the part he got went over the fence last, somebody must have given it a boost."

Maybe it was the odors sifting into the atmosphere from the direction of Ted Boynton's crackling fire. Maybe it was just curiosity, for a mud hen—although kind to its family and all—is generally about as tender and tasty as a moosehide moccasin. Anyway, there was no second call for chow that evening.

There these fowl were, brown and bulging, looking as handsome as canvasbacks and smelling no less tempting than plump ptarmigans. George C. Goodwin, American Museum mammal collector, stuck his fork gingerly into a drumstick. Steaming moist meat fell away from the bone. Everyone dug in hungrily.

"Even a loon don't cook up too bad," grins Boynton, "if a yahoo don't try to gentle it aitch-for-leather. So don't throw any of such critters away, particular in times like these. Cram them with onions. Boil real easy for three hours. Then start brand new with a crumb stuffing, tuck a mess of sow belly where it'll do the most good, and roast nice and quiet like."

More Substitutes

Substitution is a daily matter wherever men eat in farther places. When the baking soda package is empty, the bush cook knows that a like amount of white hardwood ashes will make the breadstuff rise so well that no one will be able to detect any difference. Nor is that the only kitchen use for ashes. . . .

Bread and biscuits baked in wood ashes sound dirty but are delicious. The culinary artist of the tall timbers merely rolls the kneaded dough in flour, then buries it in hot ashes to bake until a straw thrust into its middle comes out clean.

The wilderness chef recognizes, too, the value of wood ashes when the meal is over. Greasy pans practically clean themselves when boiled with them, lye turning the grease to soap. Ashes, adhering to a newly cut potato, are just the thing for shining rusty silverware.

Pick Some Spaghetti

Jokes about spaghetti growing on trees seem particularly funny to city sophisticates who have never heard that the bushman does obtain a "spaghetti" from such a source. Especially delicious in Spring is the inner bark of the beech and birch, cut into spaghetti-like strips and stewed with meat.

This spaghetti of the forests is preferred fresh by some, sundried by others. The jackpine of the Canadian Rockies furnishes a similar product which the more particular gourmets take only from the sunny side of the tree in springtime.

Syrup

The log cabin cook needs no sugar maple tree for maple syrup. A credible substitute is started by boiling six medium-sized potatoes with a couple of cups of water until one cup of fluid remains. The potatoes are removed.

Stirring the liquid until the boiling peak is again reached, the bush chef adds one cup of white sugar and another of brown. The resulting syrup, which does not taste like much at first, is bottled and resolutely put aside for several days to age. The excellence of the finished maple sugar substitute never ceases to be amazing.

Birch sap, which some backwoodsmen collect by the bucket in springtime, is used in its original state as a beverage and, when boiled down, as a table syrup.

Snow

Two tablespoons of fresh light snow will take the place of each egg in batters. The batter should be made thicker than usual to compensate for added water content. The snow should be stirred in rapidly just before cooking.

Light dry snow can also be turned into ice cream. The home manufacturer empties a can of evaporated milk into a pan, adds sugar and flavoring, and then steps outside to stir in the snow to taste.

Yankee Butter

Resourceful pioneers made Yankee butter by combining molasses with bacon drippings and other edible greases.

Bear Grease

Bear grease is a more digestible shortening than commercial lard. It may be obtained by rendering in open oven pans the incredible amount of fat with which the average black bear and grizzly is fortified by Fall.

Money-Savers

Baking soda is as good a dentifrice as most and less expensive than any of the manufactured brands. Salt is too harsh except for occasional use, but a teaspoon in a glass of water is medically regarded as equal to commercial mouth washes. A rounded teaspoon of salt in a quart of warm water is a fast-working purge when taken on an empty stomach.

Dehydrated Foods

Pemmican, buccan, parched corn, and jerky are reminders that concentrated foods played an important part in early North American days. The principle then, as now, was to extract as much moisture as possible. Whereas drying by sun and wind seldom removed more than three-fourths of the water, modern methods often leave as little as three or four per cent.

Only choicer portions are used by reputable manufacturers, eliminating necessary consumer waste entirely. Bulk and weight are radically reduced and, also an important consideration in the bush, zero temperatures are no longer threats.

Why pack twenty-five pounds of fresh pumpkin when an equivalent is a pound of powder plus twenty-four pounds of water? Legumes deshydres, as they are known in many Northeastern logging camps, are eminently satisfactory substitutes both in taste and sustenance for the fresh article. Experiments by both United States and Canadian authorities show that properly dehydrated vegetables generally retain some ninety-five per cent of the nourishment present in the freshly picked product.

Dried Eggs

One pound of some whole egg powders is the equivilent of four dozen fresh eggs. Food value is practically unchanged, but one should take care to purchase only desiccated whole, freshly laid, domestic hen eggs. Dried eggs used in cakes and puddings cannot be detected from fresh eggs.

Powdered Milk

Milk, supplying most of the thirty-four dietary substances necessary to human health, comes nearer to being an all purpose food than any other. One pound of dried whole milk has virtually the same nutritive value as one gallon of fresh milk, except for loss of Vitamin C which in this case is regarded as relatively unimportant, as milk contains only a negligible amount of this vitamin at best. Sanitary factors are often markedly superior.

Like scrambled eggs? Dissolve a tablespoon of egg powder and a teaspoon of dehydrated milk in four tablespoons of lukewarm water. Add salt, pepper, and a teaspoon of butter. Some enjoy the additional flavor of bacon grease. A little flour may be used for thickening. Scramble as usual.

Powdered Varieties

Powdered concentrates of coffee, cocoa-milk-and-sugar, soups, broths, various fruit juices, and the several vegetable salts have a definite place in wilderness living.

Saccharine, on the other hand, should not be carried unless on doctor's orders. Although sweet in flavor, it lacks energy value in which sugar excels.

Even concentrated tea is available. But who will not burden himself with a few extra ounces for the good fellowship of fire and boiling kettle, and for the pleasant ceremony of tossing a handful of palm-measured black leaves into the bubbles?

Salt

Health authorities recommend that iodized salt be used as a source of iodine unless sea food is a regular part of the diet.

Scurvy

There is seldom any need for anyone in the wilderness to have scurvy, the vitamin deficiency disease. Spruce tea, made by boiling needles of the evergreen with an equal amount of water, contains nearly as much Vitamin C as the average orange juice. Spruce tea is pleasant, too, both plain and with milk and sugar. A cup a day will keep scurvy away! Wild rose hips are also rich in Vitamin C. Plenty of rare fresh meat will, if all parts of the animal are used, also keep one safe from scurvy. Raw potatoes cost as much as a dollar apiece during the Yukon Stampede because prospectors had learned by experience that enough of them would cure scurvy. Much of this Vitamin C is lost in cooking, however.

One ounce of cevitamic acid, which is the precious Vitamin C in crystalline form, will prevent scurvy in one adult for more than one and one-half years.

Wild Foods

Starvation is no fun. The body begins living on its own flesh after a few foodless hours. The carbohydrates go first, followed by the fats. Then proteins from sinews and muscles keep the human machine functioning.

Although dread of starving is the foremost bugaboo of men caught in the North American wilderness, nearly every part of this continent abounds with wild edibles.

Tender young nettles and burdock leafstalks boil into excellent greens. Rock tripe kept part of Sir John Franklin's lost Arctic Expedition alive for weeks. Lewis and Clark found arrowhead roots "a very good substitute for bread." John Colter, fleeing from Indians, kept going on praire turnips. Groundnuts or peanuts helped the Pilgrims through their first hard winter.

No possible sustenance should be overlooked if one is in need. Shell piles beside a stream may be the clue to a mussel bed. Bees buzzing around a hollow tree often indicate that a smoky fire is in order. Frog legs are nourishing. So is snake meat. Even the riper bird eggs should not be scorned.

Rabbit-Starvation

The porcupine, like the burdock and thistle, is better fare than one might expect. The law, for one reason only, protects this mobile pin-cushion in many localities. Why? The lethargic porky is one animal that even the greenest tenderfoot can kill with a stick.

The way to prepare a porcupine is by making an incision along the smooth belly, then slipping the skin off like a glove. It's simpler, of course, to toss the carcass Indian-fashion into the fire. The quills will burn while the meat is roasting. But so will the fat! "What of it?" the cheechako may shrug.

Woodsmen know the answer. They'll remember Northerners who have died of *rabbit-starvation*. It may sound incredible that a man with all the rabbits he can eat can still die because of lack of food. It's true, nevertheless. An exclusive diet of lean meat such as rabbit will cause diarrhea within several days to a week, followed by death.

The secret is to add some fat to the lean. This will prevent the protein-poisoning. Accounts are common, nevertheless, of lost men who burn priceless fat—in frying, roasting, and other forms of high-temperature cookery—to give nutritively inferior lean meat a "better" flavor.

When starvation threatens, nothing should be cooked longer than is necessary to be palatable. The only exception is when there are germs to be destroyed. Vegetables are generally more nutritive raw. Even the practice of toasting bread decreases proteins and digestibility. The less meat is cooked, the greater is its food value.

Fish

Another fatal mistake the lost man may make is to concentrate too much time and energy on fishing. Royal Canadian Mounted Police scientists find that such fresh-water fish as perch, bass, pickerel, and pike average only 200 calories per live-pound. A man leading an active outdoor life requires upwards of 4500 calories daily!

Practices ordinarily contrary to good sportsmanship are excusable when one is lost and starving. Who can say that jigging with an unraveled thread and sharpened crotched stick is not then justified if it will produce results? Even dry-fly purists will admit cornering trout and killing them with clubs when necessity has demanded.

Fast rocky streams offer many an easy mess if one will wade along carefully and feel under the up-current sides of stones. These natural traps imprison numerous piscatory prizes. Certain Indian methods of fishing may prove lifesavers for the hungry wayfarer. One procedure is to crush the leaves and stalks of the mullein or fish weed (*croton setigerus*). These are dropped into a still pool or temporarily dammed brook. The fish therein, momentarily narcotized, will float to the surface where they should be immediately secured.

The bulbous root of the so-called soap plant (*chlorogalum pomdeidianum*) can be similarly used. So can the seeds of the southern buckeye (*aesculus pavia*). Fish caught by these emergency means are as wholesome as if merely dazed by concussion.

Feasts

Ptarmigan, grouse, partridge, and other such game birds promise feasts for those astray in the Silent Places. A stick, stone, or knot of wood is many times the only weapon needed. If one misses the first throw, the fowl will often give a second and third chance.

The alert wanderer will sometimes scare an owl from a fresh kill and a potential supper for himself. Foxes, coyotes, and wolves are also occasionally surprised at their meals. These predators almost invariably melt into the bush at the approach of a human being.

But if one comes upon a bear at its kill, it is smart to look around for a tree or exit unless one is armed and experienced. The bear, particularly if it is a black, probably won't offer any argument. Yet it may.

If you're weaponless and still need that kill enough to warrant the risk, watch your chance and build a fire beside it. Have plenty of fuel at hand, especially if night is near. And watch out. Grizzlies, for one, have a habit of dropping down close to their food.

Habits

Nearly every part of North American game animals is edible. A possible exception is polar bear liver which may be poisonous to some degree at certain times. Even gall has uses as seasoning. Blood, certainly, should not be wasted. Two ounces daily fulfill human iron requirements. It would take ten eggs to accomplish the same thing. Vital organs, too often discarded, abound with indispensable minerals and vitamins.

Hides are as nourishing as lean meat. This means that tossing a skin into a fire, as many do to burn the hair, results in a considerable amount of nutriment going up in smoke.

Eskimos depend on the salad-like contents of caribou stomachs for greens. Some Indian tribes, too, feast on the vegetable contents of herbivorous animals. A thrifty aboriginal way of preparing birds and small animals for the pot, as a matter of fact, is beating them to a pulp, entrails and all.

Taste habits become relatively unimportant when one is warding off starvation. That is why it may be profitable to remember that some Indians use rabbit excrement to thicken wild vegetable soup. Others drape unemptied deer intestines on roasting racks. Well, don't North Americans relish raw oysters, odoriferous cheeses, and whole sardines?

Bones

Cree squaws prepare a particularly invigorating dish by boiling small bones until they become gelatinous. If the creature was in good condition, the iron-rich marrow will abound in phospholipins. These humanly necessary fats are not surpassed by any other food in caloric value.

The starving man sometimes unwittingly curses old bones over which he stumbles. Yet these skeletons may mean salvation itself. They should not be roasted into friability as some Indians do but, rather, shattered and then simmered into sustaining soup.

It's true that under favorable conditions the human body can ward off starvation for one or two months by living on its own tissues. But why be a cannibal?

CHAPTER TWENTY-THREE

TRAPPER'S CABIN

Here is how a trapper's cabin was built by one man in three days for less than two dollars.

Its snugness and serviceability are attested by its long use in the Far North where "man scribbles in vain a little history, and Nature buries it in a blizzard."

No tools were employed but saw and single-edged ax. Nothing was packed in from outside but nails, spikes, two hinges, a piece of wire screen, a white cloth of similar size, and several lengths of stove pipe.

The stove pipe, being self joining, fitted neatly inside one another. A piece of rope was circled through them, and they were slung cheerfully over one shoulder. A number of old tin cans and a discarded water pail were already on the spot.

As a remote shelter for the sportsman who prefers virgin hunting and fishing to an inner-spring mattress, such a structure may well prove happy sanctuary, particularly as simple refinements can be easily added.

Site

The cabin was located among second-growth spruce a few yards back from a cut bank a hundred feet above a Canadian river. An excellent spring bubbled nearby. Firewood was plentiful and free for the taking. The site, part of the millions of square miles of public land in Canada, was open to purchase at

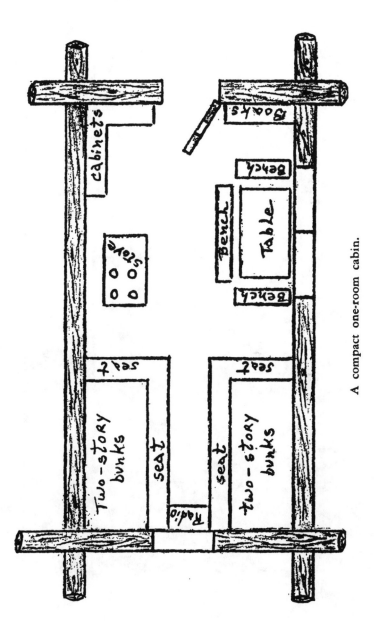

A compact one-room cabin.

289

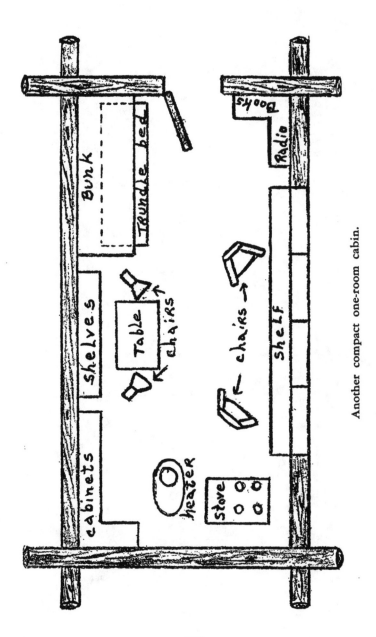

Another compact one-room cabin.

five dollars an acre. In this instance as in innumerable others, it was merely squatted upon.

Foundation

A foundation, ten feet wide and twelve feet long, was cleared amid sheltering trees on a sunny promontory on the river's north shore. An outcrop of stone bulged protectively at stormy northeast.

Mud sills were used. As the floor was to be dirt, it and the ground on which the logs were to rest were filled in to a height of several inches to assure dryness. Flat stones were embedded at the front corners.

The ax butt and the old bucket were all the pick and shovel necessary. A three-way-adjustable, folding army shovel might otherwise have been slipped into the pack.

Logs

The only demand made of the building sticks was that they be reasonably straight. The handiest trees were dropped. None was peeled. Sizes varied from poles two inches thick at the butt to logs fourteen inches through.

Spruce predominated, but some poplar was worked in. Inasmuch as all the sticks were at hand, they were felled as needed.

Base

A large dead spruce, seasoned on the stump, provided one ten-foot log and two twelve-foot logs for the base.

The former went down at the front. The latter two were angled tentatively across it. The sandstone outcrop at the rear supported the back end of each side log.

Ax cuts marked on the front log the diameter of each side log. Similar guides, indicating the width of the front log, were made on the undersides of the other two. The logs were then rolled clear and four lock notches chopped.

A tin plate of tea became the level when several fittings proved necessary before the base could be adjudged flat and square. The upper back corner of the ax head, a true right angle, provided the square. A plumb line was later improvised by knotting a string to a spike.

Walls

The walls, being only thirty inches high, went up without trouble. This being a comparatively dry country, the lock notch was used throughout. Sphagnum moss was spread generously between logs and in notches as each stick was fitted in place. The four top logs, which except at the back were the fifth of each tier, extended two feet beyond their fellows at each end.

First Ridge

Two pole supports, each seven feet long and about six inches in diameter, were spiked upright at the respective inside centers of the front and back walls.

A ridgepole, slightly flattened at each end for better contact, was spiked between their tops. The roof had been commenced. It was to be more than a foot thick.

Eave Logs

An eave log was placed between the extended back and front top logs on one side of the cabin. It was moved until poles laid experimentally over ridge and wall barely butted against its lower portions. There it was spiked into place. The process was repeated on the other side.

Inner Roof

A pole roof was loosely laid. The eave logs prevented the sticks from sliding free. Slim young spruce, averaging three inches in diameter, were used unpeeled. They were alternated, tops for butts, to compensate for tapering.

The inner roof was laid within the gables-to-be so that when the gables went up, they could be nailed to the roof poles for support. Only these four end poles were spiked into place.

Quick, The Water Bucket

Allowance was made for a stove pipe by nailing an old water bucket, the relic of a former camp, upside down in a hole made in the roof. Two long horizontal strips were nailed to the roof poles to frame the opening.

The bottom of the bucket was cut pie fashion before the utensil was shoved into place. The resulting sections were pushed outward to clamp, later, the four-inch stove pipe.

Hewing

Construction to date resembled a juvenile's sandbox; four solid sides covered by a rustic canopy.

Some planks were needed. A large dead poplar was felled. Some twenty feet of the trunk was flattened on two sides.

This was done by walking along the top and scoring with an ax; that is, making slanting cuts several inches apart. Hewing was accomplished by walking back the other way and cutting parallel to the log. This split out the chips.

Splitting

Several wedges, a foot long and similar in shape to an ax head, were chopped from a limb of the dead poplar.

A four-foot section was sawed off the flattened piece of the poplar trunk. The edge of the ax was centered against one end of the short log. Its butt was hammered with a billet. A crack appeared along the middle of the log. It was extended by pounding in wedges until the log split into two crude planks. These were smoothed somewhat with an ax.

Doorway

Two poles were nailed temporarily to the cabin front to guide the sawing of the door opening and also to hold the severed logs in place.

The bottom log was flattened along the top to provide an outward-slanting sill.

The two hewn pieces, each four feet high, were spiked to the sides. The doorway became two feet wide. The guide poles were then pried off.

Gables

The gables were filled in roughly with odds and ends, each stick being spiked to the outer poles of the roof. These sticks extended roughly two feet beyond the inner roof of poles.

Reluctant Window

When the gable in front had been laid up to the top of the door frame, two guide poles were nailed in place. A window opening was then reluctantly sawed. It was eighteen inches square when framed at each side by hewn planks.

The same gable log that topped the window became the upper part of the door frame. It was flattened at this latter span before being secured.

The bit of wire screen was later nailed over the outside of the window opening. A white cloth covered it for warmth. A slight rent was made in the latter, a grudging concession to visibility.

Door

The door was made of hewn planks, backed by flattened poles arranged in a Z. When it was later hinged in place, small quartered poles nailed to the jamb made a frame against which it fitted when shut.

The door opened inside the cabin. The inside lock consisted of a wooden peg slanted behind it into the jamb. Looping an attached wire over a nail outside fastened the door when the camp was vacated.

Shaping Gables

Poles nailed to the gables indicated the pitch of the final roof. The gables were then sawed with the poles as guides.

The gables at this stage did not reach to the top of what was to be the final roof. These triangular spaces were eventually sheathed with spruce bark.

Purlins

Four purlins were set in steps cut in the gables. They were arranged so that poles angled across them and the top wall logs butted into the eave log, yet were eighteen inches above the inner pole roof at the ridge.

Each purlin extended three feet beyond the gables. After being fitted, they were taken down for the time being.

Insulation

Quantities of bark were spread over the orginal pole roof. Then dry grass, leaves, and spruce boughs were heaped on. After the purlins had been spiked in position, moist clay was pressed into place.

A second pole roof, similar to the first, was butted loosely into the eave logs. Only the four end sticks were spiked.

Shakes

Shakes, nailed to light flattened poles that extended across the roof parallel to the ridge, completed the roof. This addition made the top practically waterproof.

The shakes were made two feet long and about eight inches wide. They were lapped only three inches, so as to avoid over-exertion.

The shakes were rived from two-foot sections sawed from spruce that had died on the butt. Each chunk was split, then quartered. The ax head was held in position again, hammered with a billet of firewood, and the quarters became eighths, and then sixteenths.

The thick outer edges of the shakes were left rounded. The inner edges were trimmed wherever they had become too thin.

Flashing Ridge

Once the shakes were in place, birch bark was spread over the ridge and fastened on both sides by nailed strips of wood for that final weather-proofing touch. The makeshift stove pipe thimble was flashed as tightly as possible with flattened tin cans.

Chinking

Moss had been spread liberally between all sticks and in all joints as building had progressed. The cabin had a bewhiskered aspect.

Clay, moistened to the consistency of putty, was plastered into the crevices where the moss helped to bind it. One of the erstwhile wedges was used for pressing and smoothing the mud into place. A damp cloth removed any rough particles remaining.

Stove

Two sections of seven-inch stove pipe were interlocked to make the heater described in Chapter Seventeen. This was set on the dirt floor in a pen of rocks and clay.

The four-inch smoke pipe was extended through the water-bucket thimble. The new materials smoked a bit when a fire was kindled, but the stove proved to draw well. A rubbabou of flour, water, and rabbit was put on to simmer for supper.

Bunk

One pole six feet long, four poles each half that length, and a few nails were all that was needed to install a bunk frame in one corner. A number of limber green saplings were nailed lengthwise to make the venerable pole spring of the wilderness. An ax load of spruce boughs provided the sparse but aromatic mattress.

Finalities

Hewn planks, supported by brackets made by sawing rectangular slabs diagonally, became shelves. Other planks afforded that ultimate in trapper luxury, a spot of wooden floor to caress stockinged feet on frosty mornings.

CHAPTER TWENTY-FOUR

BLOCKHOUSE

The wilderness dweller seeking a different log home, yet one in keeping with the early North American tradition, may well consider the blockhouse.

This frontier motif may be authentically carried to extents limited by little but energy. The bastion may even involve a stockade and a heavily barred gate reached by a drawbridge.

What outdoor play house—if children have been clamoring for one—could equal a blockhouse constructed in miniature?

Design

The simplest design is the square. Pioneer blockhouses, being built by human beings, varied in form. Many were four sided, while others had six or more walls.

Loopholes

The fact that the blockhouse of old boasted loopholes more often than windows does not mean that the modern version should not have plenty of the latter. The illusion may be retained by the use of heavy shutters. Holes, which in centuries past might have admitted the muzzle of flintlock or matchlock, may be bored in these shutters and then whittled to give them a hand-made appearance.

Dimensions

The smaller the bastion within reason, the easier it will be to build. A lower room 12 feet square will often prove sufficient, inasmuch as additional sleeping and living quarters will be afforded by the upstairs. This upper room may be 16 feet square. Neither story need be higher than seven feet.

Materials

Logs may be used throughout. Most builders, however, will find poles, slabs, and similar light rustic materials easier to handle for the upper story.

Construction

The tenon corner, easily and accurately made by saw alone, is an apt one for this work.

The four top wall logs may be square notched by saw and chisel and extended for whatever distances the upper story is to be superimposed. Reinforcing both sets with parallel logs of similar length will provide a solid footing for the second floor.

Roof

Recommendatory is the flat roof, both because of comparative ease of construction and because of suitability as a sun deck and observation platform. Instead of an ordinary railing, poles and slabs may be used to suggest battlements.

Door

The more massive the door, the more harmonious it will be. Here is the place for heavy hewn planks, studded with nails approximating hand wrought varieties as closely as possible.

Lock

The door may fittingly be secured on the inside by a stout wooden bar. This may be conveniently centered by nut and bolt to the door itself, so that it may be turned as illustrated into wooden guards at the sides.

Two latch strings can be attached, one to pull the balanced bar shut and the other to release it. The ends of these strings may be tied to clinched nails and the latter pushed inconspicuously into holes so that there will be nothing to distinguish them from or-

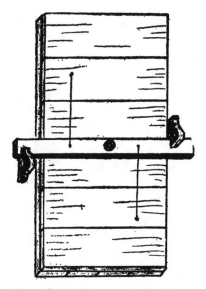

Door bar with two latchstrings.

dinary nails. Uninitiated passersby would find the mystery harder
to solve than a commercial lock.

Access

A ladder to the upper room will satisfy a few, although a stairway backed by cabinets and shelves will be preferred by most. A
rugged effect can be achieved by using a huge slanted log in
which steps have been sawed. It would be well to provide a pole
railing with this.

A trapdoor for the hole in the floor of the second story will afford both heat control and privacy.

If there is to be a trapdoor to the roof, it may be hinged to fit
like a lid over a raised and flashed frame. Here is an opportunity,
too, for a combination exit and skylight.

Heat

Heat from the ground floor may generally be counted upon to
warm the second room, particularly if the stove pipe is run

through these latter quarters and fitted with a drum oven. The latter will provide auxiliary cooking facilities of a sort for the backwoods duplex.

Stockade Plus

The modern stockade may be but a partial stretch of pickets for service as a wind break, or it may be an olden enclosure with barred gate and even an observation gallery running along the inside. Some friendly bush may hide a secret postern. Then one day earth will fly. Before the woodland brook realizes what is happening, it will be diverted to fill a moat. Weights and pulleys may be adjusted so that a pole drawbridge can be raised and lowered at almost a finger's touch.

CHAPTER TWENTY-FIVE

TODAY IS FIRE

"For two years I lived alone in the woods in a house which I built myself. I am convinced by experience that to maintain oneself on this earth is not a hardship but a pastime, if we live simply and wisely."

So wrote Henry David Thoreau a century ago—in rugged sentences whose significance grows with the years, as what is called an advancing civilization becomes increasingly frenzied and complex.

"I went to the woods because I wanted to live deep and suck out all the marrow of life."

Time For Living

"The exact cost of my house was $28.12.

"I spaded up all the land which I required for my beans, potatoes, corn, peas and turnips. I learned that if one would live simply and eat only the crop he raised, and raise no more than he ate, he would need to cultivate only a few rods of ground.

"He could do all his necessary farm work as it were with his left hand at odd hours in the summer. It is not necessary that a man should earn his living by the sweat of his brow, unless he sweats easier than I do. My food alone cost me in money about twenty-seven cents a week.

"Most men live mean lives, always on the limits; trying to get out of debt; making themselves sick, that they may lay up something against a sick day.

"I learned from my experience that it would cost incredibly little trouble to obtain one's necessary food; that a man may use as simple a diet as the animals, and yet retain health and strength. "As for clothing, a man who has found something to do will not need a new suit to do it in."

Adventures In Simplicity

"When I took up my abode in the woods, every morning was a cheerful invitation to make my life of equal simplicity with Nature herself. I got up as the sun arose, and bathed in the pond, while the mists, like ghosts, were stealthily withdrawing in every direction into the woods. It was a religious exercise, and one of the best things which I did.

"I had this advantage in my mode of life over those who were obliged to look abroad for amusement—that my life itself was become my amusement and never ceased to be novel."

Fall

"By September, two or three small maples turned scarlet across the pond. Gradually from week to week the character of each tree came out, and it admired itself in the smooth mirror of the lake.

"When chestnuts were ripe I laid up half a bushel for winter. It was exciting to roam the woods with a bag on my shoulder.

"It was in November that I first began to inhabit my house, when I began to use it for warmth as well as shelter. It did me good to see the soot form on the back of the chimney which I had built, and I poked the fire with more satisfaction than usual."

Winter

"When freezing weather came I plastered the walls. At length the winter set in in good earnest, just as I had finished, and the terrestrial music of the wind began to howl around the house as if it had not had permission to do so till then.

"Night after night the geese came lumbering in with a clangor and a whistling of wings, even after the ground was covered with snow.

"My employment out of doors now was to collect the dead

wood in the forest, sometimes trailing a dead pine tree under each arm to my shed.

"When the snow lay deepest no wanderer ventured near my house for a fortnight at a time, but there I lived as snug as a meadow mouse. In the morning I would take an axe and pail and go to the pond in search of water.

"Cutting my way through snow and then ice, I open a window under my feet, where, kneeling to drink, I look down into the quiet parlor of the fishes, pervaded by a softened light as through ground glass. There a perennial waveless serenity reigns as in the twilight sky. Heaven is under our feet as well as over our heads."

Spring

"The first sparrow of spring! The year beginning with younger hope than ever! The faint silvery warblings heard over the bare, moist fields from the bluebird and the redwing, as if the last flakes of winter tinkled as they fell!

"The sinking sound of melting snow is heard in all dells, and the ice dissolves space in the ponds. The grass flames up on the hillsides like a spring fire, as if the earth sent forth an inward heat to greet the returning sun."

Tonic

"We need the tonic of wildness—to wade sometimes in marshes where the bittern and the meadow hen lurk, and hear the booming of the snipe; to smell the whispering sedge where only some wilder and more solitary fowl builds her nest, and the mink crawls with its belly close to the ground.

"We can never have enough of nature. We must be refreshed by the sight of inexhaustible vigor, vast and titanic features, the wilderness with its living and its decaying trees, the thundercloud, the rain."

You

You, certainly, are not going to be one of those who spends "the best part" of his life "earning money in order to enjoy a questionable liberty during the least valuable part of it!"

If the call of the outdoors rings loudly for you, why not take the first blow at civilization's shackles while senses are keen and muscles vigorous? Why not make the first move now, even if it is only to acquire a retreat in nearby woods, where you can have at least "weekend intimacy with God?"

Your Wilderness Home

"If one advances confidently in the direction of his dreams and endeavors to live the life he has imagined, he will meet with success unexpected in common hours," Thoreau learned.

"If you have built castles in the air, your work need not be lost. That is where they should be. Now put the foundations under them."

Even if the gratifying actuality of building the wilderness home cannot be commenced for months, anybody can begin immediately to savor some of the most delightful pleasures of all. . . . The thrill of planning! The excitement of thumbing maps and books! The joy of drawing queer designs with stubby pencils on notebooks kept handy for when inspiration comes!

BUILD IT NOW!

"Yesterday is ashes, tomorrow wood," so the Indians say. "Only today does the fire burn brightly."

THE END

INDEX

INDEX